6.95

WYOMING:

Rugged but Right

Dedicated to the ones I love the most . . . .
Rita, Laura, Bob, Barbara, Betty . . . and Wyoming, as well as Vickie, Tom, Tim, Peter,
Katy, and Bobby!

WYOMING:

Rugged but Right

By

William F. Bragg, Jr.

Foreword by Robert W. "Red" Fenwick

PRUETT PUBLISHING COMPANY
Boulder, Colorado

ISBN: 0-87108-539-9 hard
ISBN: 0-87108-540-2 soft

Library of Congress Catalog Card No. 79-3527

First Edition

2 3 4 5 6 7 8 9

Photographs on pages 6, 15, 40, 50, 70, 89, 100, 107, 113, 132, 134, 135, 158-159, 170-171, 176-177, are reproduced through the courtesy of the Western History Research Center, University of Wyoming, Laramie.

Photographs on pages 30, 33, 53, 55, 56, 64-65, 86, 103, 104, 114, 130, 145, 174, and 178 are reproduced through the courtesy of the Wyoming State Archives, Museums and Historical Department.

Line drawings by Bill Dickerson furnished through the courtesy of Guaranty Federal Savings and Loan Association, Casper, Wyoming.

Photograph on P. 168 reproduced through the courtesy of the State of Utah, Dept. of Development Services.

Cover painting by Conrad Schwiering

Printed in the United States of America

Foreword By Robert W. (Red) Fenwick

It's a curious, widely accepted fact that coffee, flapjacks, bacon and eggs cooked over a campfire and flavored with wood ashes, taste infinitely better and are more handily digestible than the same vittles prepared in the finest restaurants.

Of course, the quality of the grub is further enhanced if it's cooked by a grumpy, short-fused despot of the pots and pans who knows how to drive a wagon, "rope wood" and wash dishes in sand when the water's short. That takes experience and many miles of trail dust.

There's an elusive something about the two — good trail cookin' and cranky cooks — that's synonymous: Both have authority.

At least that's my opinion, and I feel the same way about historians and their writings about the West and its oldtimers, its mountain men, Indians, pioneers, homesteaders, ranchers and rustlers, cowhands, railroaders, gaudy ladies, gamblers and gunmen.

To me, a western historian has to have "authority." He has to have ridden the trails, rubbed shoulders at the bar with many an old gaffer, hunkered down by the barn, or on the cattle trail with a few cowpunchers, ranchmen and sheepherders, before he can write with authority.

Just such an historian is my old and valued friend, Bill Bragg, Jr., author of this here new book about our home state, titled *Wyoming: Rugged But Right!*

Bill's book has "authority." Its fascinating little vignettes of early life and people in Wyoming is fragrant with the incense of burning pine and sagebrush and the refreshing, nostril-tingling tang of forest breezes and winds from the broad, sweeping vistas of open rangeland.

Wyoming: Rugged But Right! pulsates with the beat of war drums, the thunder of cavalry in the charge, and the wild ululations of Indians and mountain men at the rendezvous. He tells how many there were in Wyoming, and where they were.

Bill Bragg's living, breathing storyettes of life on the frontier, humanize history and bring its characters into sharper focus.

From a gifted sire who earned national acclaim for his western fiction, Bill Jr., inherited a way with words and a love of Wyoming ferocious as a grizzly's affection for her cubs. And, pal, never come between a grizzly and her cubs or between Bill Bragg and his Wyoming. That's a fair warning.

You have to know a little bit about Bragg, the author, historian, one-time prize-fighter, U.S. Marine in World War II, history teacher at Casper Junior College:

He's the kind of guy who likes to listen to others talk — if they have something to say. If they don't, they'll soon discover that Bill is a pretty good talker, himself.

Bill is blessed with an exceptionally retentive mind. He also has the ability to know a "story" when he hears it and to separate the commonplace from the unusual. That's why Bill's book contains so many previously untold tales, exciting, warmly human yarns.

A researcher, Bill has checked out most of the uncommon accounts of the frontier. And if the story is fable, he'll tell you so.

Therefore it's not surprising to learn that Wyatt Earp actually acquired his skill with a gun in Wyoming; that women first served in the U.S. Army at Fort D.A. Russell in 1890, and much more.

In Bill's book you'll meet Gen. Crook's Jackass Army; the ghost of old Fort Laramie; a Scot nobleman who perhaps introduced the first American Indians to the British Isles; an early-day newspaper reporter whose articles never were published but who wrote about Cheyenne that he'd seen "one shooting, three hangings and a blizzard in 24 hours," and Orphansent Fish whose story you'll never believe.

You'll read about Casper, Wyoming's unusual ordinance about women and their behavior between the hours of 7 A.M. and 10 P.M., and Poker Nell and the madames of Deadwood, S.D.

And you'll thrill as I did to accounts of bandits on the Cheyenne-Deadwood Stagecoach Line, the Hole-in-the-Wall Country, and an oldtime, frontier sheriff named Malcolm Campbell.

Bill told me several years ago he'd assembled notes on little, intimate tales about early Wyoming that he'd heard around the state, and said "If I write 'em in a book, will you write the prologue?"

He did and I did, and here it is. I'm sure you'll like it.

Introduction

This is a collection of tales, legends, true and unusual stories, bizarre, funny, and different yarns of old Wyoming. In my opinion as a native son of Wyoming whose family were territorial pioneers, these stories help make up the great tapestry we call the history of Wyoming. We cannot let them slide away into oblivion. They must be saved and savored for the generations yet to come. These are not the paragraphs you will read in the staid history of the State being tramped out in the vineyards of learning by prim eastern college professors. These are the stories of what it really was like in Wyoming, when how a man used a shovel, a maul, and a six shooter was more important than how he dressed and how he handled his eatin' irons and tools at a banquet given by the local banker.

One must realize that these stories are but a few of the many told to me by old-timers, or by their offspring or close friends. I've had to very carefully select these stories because for each one, there are variations of it, I'm certain, rattling around in some family trunk or attic.

Thus, these are a few of the stories I firmly believe to be a mortal part of the soul of Wyoming. . . . I only hope that those who take the time to read this collection of tales agree with me.

I have to thank the University of Wyoming Archives, the Archives, Museum, and Historical Department in Cheyenne, and Jerry Keenan, the editor at Pruett Publishing for their lasting belief in me and this book of Wyoming yarns. Thanks are also due to both the Casper College and Natrona County libraries and the staff of each library. I want to thank Bill Dickerson for his work in the fine line drawings, and I take great personal pride in saying my thanks to James D. Sprecher and Guaranty Federal Savings and Loan Association in Casper, who own the Dickerson drawings and loaned them to me for use in this book. I know Jim Sprecher will like what this book stands for, because like me he is a member of a pioneer territorial family, and as such, knows those values set down in the early days in young Wyoming will help the State to carry on and survive through the present population boom.

How can one say thanks to a man like Connie Schwiering? His paintings are recognized the world over for their sharp, bright, clean strokes telling the story of the Tetons, and Jackson Hole — yes — and Wyoming in bright colors that run riot across the canvas now being preserved in homes, in office buildings, and art museums around the world. His stories about his love of his home state stand forth boldly everywhere you look, and we are honored and proud he let us use one of his works of art for the cover of this book.

And, finally, Red Fenwick. . .and who hasn't read those great columns "Ridin' The Range With Red Fenwick," seen for years and years in *The Denver Post?* Another native son — from Douglas — Red Fenwick is the friend of Bill Bragg. That should say it all between those two. And it does. But for those who don't understand that kind of feeling, let it be said by the author to this book, "What Schwiering does with paint, Fenwick does with a typewriter. How the hell can I lose on this book with two of Wyoming's greatest artists lending their support to the effort?"

William F. Bragg, Jr.
Casper, Wyoming

Part One
First Citizens

Who Were the Sioux?

Generally speaking, it was the Sioux Indians who played the most important and vital roles in the history of the West. Thus, it might be well to learn a little about this great nation of Indians.

The Sioux was the largest nation of Indians in America. In the main, it consisted of seven great divisions: the Medewacanton, or village of spirit lake; the Wahpacoota, or leaf shooters; the Wahpeton, or leaf village; the Siseston, or swamp village; the Yankton, or end village; the Yanktonais, or upper end village; and the Teton, or prairie village people.

These seven divisions stretched at one time all the way from central Wisconsin to the Yellowstone-Jackson region in Wyoming. The Teton Sioux made up more than two-thirds of the total Sioux nation.

The Teton Sioux are again divided into seven divisions. The Brule, or burnt thighs; the Oglala, meaning scattering of dust in the face — or bad faces; Hunkpapa, meaning those who camp at the end of the camping circle; the Itazipka, meaning without bows, or Sans Arc; the Minikanzu, or those who plant by the water; the Sihasapa, or black feet (not to be confused with the Blackfeet Indians in Montana); and finally, the Ohenonpa, or two kettle tribe. It is reckoned that following the Wounded Knee Massacre in 1890, when the last big battle was fought in the West, that there were 24,000 Sioux Indians living on the High Plains.

The Teton Sioux were nomads and buffalo hunters, and those who came in direct contact with them in the West before the turn of the century said that they were a superior race of redmen — dignified, stately, and warlike.

Sitting Bull, Red Cloud, Crazy Horse, Roman Nose, Spotted Tail, Yellow Knife, Gall, American Horse, Short Bull, Old Man Afraid of His Horses — these are some of the better known Teton

Sioux leaders who have come to grace the pages of our history. These are the red men who took war parties past Casper on their way south to the Denver area, or led charges on Fetterman and Custer.

Imagine yourself a young Teton warrior getting ready for a buffalo hunt in the Gillette area of Wyoming about 125 years ago. Runners would be sent to all the lodges reporting a grand hunt was to be organized. You would daub yourself in paint, rub down your best pony and ready your bow and arrows for the festive occasion. Young boys would have already ridden out to find the herd, and after they had raced their horses back with the news of the location of the herd, you would ride in a stately fashion, your mother, wife, and sisters on foot behind you until you neared the buffalo.

Then the fun of the hunt would begin, and as you killed a buffalo the female members of your family would run in to strip the hide off the carcass, cut out the choice chunks of meat, save the hide from the neck (this was the toughest part of the hide and made good shields and moccasins) and then return to the camp.

Your work would be over. But the women would work far into the night making jerked meat by cutting the meat into thin strips and letting them dry and cure. They would also roast fresh chunks of buffalo for you to enjoy along with the other hunters. Finally, the women would make pemmican out of the jerked meat by pounding it into a hash with a stone hammer. Then the bones would be cracked and the marrow removed by boiling the bones until the grease or marrow rose to the surface. When it cooled, the marrow was skimmed off the surface and poured over the pounded meat. As soon as the mixture cooled, it was sewed into leather bags or buried in order to preserve it for lean times in the future. Years later Arctic explorers found pemmican a lifesaver on numerous occasions.

And while you were a proud member of the Teton Sioux, other tribes would call you a "cutthroat," that is, when referring to your tribe by hand signals, they would make a sign of throat cutting. This would not mean you were actually a cutthroat, it would refer to a shell-like necklace most Teton Sioux wore around their necks.

In the summer and on the plains you would live in a buffalo hide tepee. If you traveled into the Jackson-Yellowstone or Big Horn mountain region where you liked to summer, fish, and hunt, you would live in a tree and bark tepee.

Above all else, you were preeminently a wandering buffalo

hunter — and on occasion — a proud and fierce warrior. And you would listen to the singers and medicine men and know they were right when they sang this song:

In a sacred manner I live
To the heavens I gazed
In a sacred manner I live
My horses are many.

Cheyenne Indian Paint

Every once in awhile I am caught in some conversation with a bright young thing whose main topic in life is painting. As I listen, I ask her where she gets her paint? Then, I steer the conversation to the Cheyenne Indians and painting, and getting the floor I tell her about how those bright people lived, and what and how they painted.

You know something? The kids I talk to really are interested, so I thought you might want to learn how the Indians made their paint.

Green, the color for life, was made from dried water plants, from algae, boiled rotten wood, and earth, which we now know contained copper ore.

Yellow came from yellow clay, ground up buffalo gall stones, pine tree moss, and certain boiled vine roots.

Browns came from gum covered cottonwood tree buds, and from certain clays.

Red, looking at many of our own mountains containing oxides of iron, you would know this was used as well as certain clays and various boiled roots.

Black came from charcoal mixed with yellow dirt and tallow with a mixture of bast, which is the roasted inner bark of trees.

White came from chalklike dirt and clays with ground-up kaolin, which is really an aluminum silicate, although the Indians did not know it.

Blue was derived from duck droppings, from blue mud, from what we now call bentonite and from boiled rotten wood.

Each color meant a different thing — yellow for perfection or growing; black for dull, not glowing any more or death; white meaning movement or action; red for warmth; green for growing things; blue for serenity and the blue sky; and various combinations meant other things, too.

When white man first came, one of the things he carried most prized by Indians were trade beads of different colors. Later, white man came with all sorts of commercial colors to which the Indian responded in absolute delight.

Most white people assume that red men just smeared the paint on in a haphazzard manner, but the real truth is that each color, each streak, each line carried real significance just as each feather the Indian wore told a different story.

After smearing the body with the fat taken from buffalo back fat, the dry paint, which had been carried in small buckskin bags, was moistened by tongue or by finger dipped into water, and then applied with a feather tip, a small stick, or the finger. The fat or oil held the paint in place.

One other item white man brought that added to the body painting was a mirror. Every Indian wanted a small mirror, the better with which he or she could apply the paint themselves.

Of course, designs on lodges, horses, shields, arrows, lances, and clothing were painted — and in every tribe a painting guild or cult prescribed how to use paint, find it, make it, and how to apply it to the surface of whatever object was to be decorated.

By now, I would have half way converted a bright young thing from cubism and modern painting to want to try to find a half dozen buffalo gall stones, some clay, blueberries, and pine tree bark so she could delve into the mysteries of prehistoric painting of the first Americans.

Women's Guilds Among the Cheyenne

Each nation of people devise their own rules of conduct, how they intend to fight to preserve their way of life, and organize themselves at various levels so that all segments of their people sooner or later find a place to function and serve.

Cheyenne Indians were no different. They had six or seven societies for their men, a number for their women, and rules grew out of each group that led to a sort of governing body that held sway over their tribe.

If the women did not belong to one group, they could join another, or be invited to join a guild. One of the most important was the Quilling Society or Guild.

Work done for ceremonial decorations had to be taught by the Quilling Guild, especially since the object would be decorated with porcupine quills. Work done in fulfillment of a vow should be done in a prescribed way outlined by Quilling Guild members. In fact, if a woman wanted to become a member of this guild she had to do a ceremonial work of art under the guidance of the Quilling Guild, then offer it for inspection, and if accepted, she too, became a member of this rigidly controlled women's guild.

Other women's guilds were for working on cornstalks used in medicine dances; learning the use of feathers in terms of types of birds from which they came, how to fletch them to arrows, and how to use them as mystic, secret, or colorful ornaments. Beadworking was another guild. These women were taught by the beadworking guild how to lay out designs, what the symbols meant, and the manner in which they were to be used, and by whom. Finally another important woman's guild was the one that did the painting of lodges, shields, clothing, arrows, and the making of the colors to be used, and why they were used.

Speaking of colors, women in the painting guild learned that white was to be used for active life; black for slowing down of hostilities; red for warmth and home and food; blue for serenity; yellow for ripeness; green for life; and that combinations of the colors could mean other things.

I have always liked their reasoning behind the color chart and reasons for their use — black from a dead fireplace meaning lifeless; white meaning action, or blurred movement; red from warmth, cooking over the fire, and home; blue for the sky and serenity; green, of course, from green growing things, or life; and yellow from perfection or growing or ripeness or from the sunsets or sunrises.

So — women among the Cheyenne had other things to do besides playing *ba-qati,* their game much like monopoly today, raising children, and running the household, or tepee lodge. They too, like our women today, belonged to clubs and carried on with their guild or club programs for the good of their families, their communities, and their souls.

The Religious Cheyenne

For all their warrior cults, and their splendid bravery the Cheyenne were among the most religious of the Plains Indians.

Their tribal history, as far back as they could remember, was tied to great mystic personages who appeared in visions before them, gave them their unity, their name, and explained how to live, what to eat, and how to observe religious ceremonies.

Every animal, fish, or bird had a religious beginning, and some that did not actually exist were still felt to live as did the others.

I am talking about the thunderbird now. This imaginary bird was as alive to the Cheyenne as the eagle is to you and I that we see soaring across Wyoming landscapes today. For the Cheyenne, the thunderbird was a great bird whose shadow was the thunder clouds, and whose flapping wings caused the thunder.

From his eyes, the thunderbird threw bolts of lightning to the ground destroying trees, killing horses, buffalo, and occasionally an Indian. His image, created on walls, drawn on tepee lodges, and cut on strips of leather, carried a special meaning to the Cheyenne.

The Cheyenne composed many songs about the thunderbird, and one went this way:

I circle around —
I circle around —
The boundaries of the earth,
Wearing the long wing feathers as I fly.

In their world, which was considered a slender disk, the Cheyenne were often visited by spirits they knew of, had heard of, and were terrifying when they came.

One such spirit was the eclipse of 1878. The total eclipse of the sun brought the Henry Draper Eclipse Expedition to Wyoming with Tom Edison as a part of the long line of world-famous astronomers from Prussia, Russia, Great Britain, France, and the United States.

When the men gathered near Rawlins at Separation Point to observe the heavenly phenomenon, the Indians thought their world had come to an end when their father the sun hid his face from them.

From the depths of depression among Indians during the eclipse some gained great power. One such was a young Piaute in Nevada on the Walker River who had the foresight to predict the eclipse.

When the eclipse came off as Wovoka said it would, as he had seen it in his dreams, he gained power as a messiah, and eventually it was this man who created the Ghost Dance Religion, which ended December 29, 1890, in front of the blazing guns of the U.S. Army at Wounded Knee.

Such was the power Indians gained from time to time from their religious symbols and beliefs, that whole tribes and nations would follow one man to their death as happened in the case of Wovoka, who promised them no bullets could harm them if they wore leather shirts painted with mysterious and religious symbols he had seen in his dream when he forecast the eclipse.

Games Played By the Cheyenne

Tsona, or the awl game, was probably the most popular game played by the Plains Indians. I should have said, by Plains Indian women, because men did not play it.

After all, an awl was a needle and what would a soldier or warrior use a needle for?

Anyway, the awl game was played on a large buffalo robe with the hair side turned to the ground. Squared, it was pegged down at all four corners and then at each corner an inverted half moon was drawn with three dots stretching to the middle where two lines were drawn and then three more dots and another inverted half moon at the next corner. This design was repeated all the way around the four sides of the hide, or playing platform.

Four sticks with various designs painted on them were the playing sticks, which were thrown into the middle of the hide and a score counted up depending on which side and in what order the sticks fell. The woman throwing the sticks would take her needle, or awl, and start on her side of the game sticking the awl first into the three dots, using both corners of the inverted crown and on around, taking as many moves as the number came to that was figured from the sticks she had thrown in the first place.

If her awl landed upon another person or awl, then that person had to start all over again. If, by chance her awl fell upon one of the straight lines between the three dots on all four sides of the hide, then she would have figuratively fallen into a river and would have to "swim" as it were, back to the starting point. If, again by chance the number cast placed her awl upon the bank of a wiggly line drawn showing a river, this meant she has drowned and she lost the game.

In some tribes, women were only allowed to play the game once in awhile because some became so addicted to the gambling side of it that they would chance their tepee lodge, horses, and sometimes you could read where a woman lost her man with a bad throw in the *tsona*, or awl game!

Kids had a sort of top they spun. They made small editions of bows and arrows. And, while the Indian never really developed the wheel, they did develop it as a rolling hoop for target practice.

One game the children had was a bull roarer. They would take a flat piece of wood about six inches long, notched on the edges and painted colorfully. Attached to it was a buckskin string about three feet long. Whirl it rapidly around your head, and from it comes a sort of roaring sound, or humming sound.

All kids played with a shinny stick, and a leather covered ball. Goals set up on each end of a playing field where one team tried to push the ball through in order to score a point sounds a little like our own games today.

Another game both men and women could play together was *mon shimuh*. This means throwing or striking against, and if you guessed it was dice, you would be right. The dice were oval shaped, not square like ours, but the principle was the same, and from what I could learn, the stakes were high.

The Vanishing American

I stood on the lip of Washakie Reservoir the other day and talked with Jack Hereford, chief law enforcement officer of the Tribal Council of the Arapaho and Shoshone Indians, on game and fish matters on the huge and beautiful Wind River Indian Reservation.

We discussed the efforts both tribes were taking in caring for the game and fish and birds and their land as opposed to their lack of care twenty-five years before. And, he understood that this 520,000 acres of land was a very valuable piece of real estate and knew its towering mountains, its streams, its birds, fish, animals, and above all its Indian heritage, would become more valuable with the passing of each day.

And then we got to talking about the old American theory of the "Vanishing American." We knew about it. It sort of starts with the seventeenth-century tune — ten little, nine little, eight little

Indians — seven little, six little, five little Indians — four little, three little, two little Indians — one little Indian boy.

You remember that tune. Simple as it is, it says Indians are going to vanish. And people like a Supreme Court Justice named Joseph Story in 1828 said about the Indian, "What can be more melancholy than their history?" And then he answered his own question by saying, "They seem destined to a slow but sure extinction. Everywhere," he said, "at the approach of white man, they fade away. We can hear the rustling of their footsteps, like that of withered leaves of autumn, and they are gone forever. They pass mournfully by and they return no more."

That was 1828 — and a few years later we started to remove them from the path of the white man and followed the seclusion by exclusion theory hoping they would survive. And, at the same time we were fighting them in the West, killing off their food supply — the buffalo — and then putting them on reservations, following again the theory of seclusion by exclusion. This was finally typified by Fraser's stone monument — "The End of The Trail" — of the warrior on the tired pony, the warrior slumped forward, his lance and shield at rest.

Ralph Waldo Emerson said, "We see in the Indians only as a picturesque antiquity — Squantum, Nantuket, Narragansett. But where are the men?"

Slowly, but surely, the idea of a vanishing race has come to a slowing down process. Those who have been on reservations are now assuming more and more care about the tribe, and they are doing it through the tribal council, and red power is rearing up, and the American Indian Movement has for its statue a powerful Indian on a rearing horse with his lance and shield at the ready.

In the process of showing the rest of America that they are not a vanishing race, red men all over the United States are painting, writing, holding public office and learning to manage their tribal affairs with grace, with good heart, and with the same serious attitude they once felt before the buffalo were all gone.

It is good, and most Indians do not want demonstrations. They want to manage their affairs, develop their reservations, their ranches, their schools, and take as active a part as that young Indian did in the affairs of the United States of America who helped raise Old Glory on Iwo Jima. I know Jack Hereford agrees; you see, he is a veteran of World War II and of the Korean War, and if anyone is all-American it is a guy named Jack Hereford. He is real — not a Vanished American.

The Papoose Tree

Of all of the strange stories I ever heard, I would guess one of the strangest was the so-called Papoose Tree at Fort Laramie.

It was an Indian burial tree for the babies that died there. One Indian burial custom called for the pyre or scaffold burial. That is where the body is wrapped in deerskin, or some animal hide along with personal objects like a prized button, piece of mirror, favorite bow and the like, and finally, placed on a wooden scaffold.

The closest member to the deceased keeps an eye on the body for a length of time. Then, one dark night, the body is secretly removed and taken a long distance from that place and given a cache burial.

This means that the body is placed, usually beside the bank of a small stream. The person carrying out this ritual cuts a round lid out of the sod and lifts it carefully out, placing the sod lid on a stretched out buffalo robe, so no traces of grass or dirt will remain once the hole is cut into the earth. Dirt is also piled onto the robe.

When a good sized hole is dug out, willows — also cut from a distant place — are used to line the hole and finally, the body and prized possessions are eased into the hole. The dirt is put back into the hole, and the lid firmly tamped back in place like the lid on a Halloween pumpkin. Remaining dirt is flapped off the robe into the stream and thus, all evidence of a grave or burial is removed and the spirit of the dead one, according to the Indians, can then peacefully join his or her ancestors.

Of course, there were other types of burials among the Indians. One such was the crevasse, or crack burial, wherein the body is allowed to slide into a crack in a canyon wall and tons of dirt and rock pried into it.

Still, the idea of using a big cottonwood tree for the burial of a dead child or papoose is not often mentioned in the annals of the American frontier.

Across the Laramie River at old Fort Laramie stood several very large cottonwood trees with limbs stretching almost to the sky. Mrs. Burt, wife of the post Commandant, said that at one time she counted over forty papoose burials in the limbs of each tree. Since the Indians were on the move, many of them never got back to perform the ancient cache burial rite, and the papoose body stayed there for many weeks until it finally dropped to the ground where the coyotes, crows, and magpies finished off the remains. Mrs. Burt said as much as she would have liked to do something about those that fell, it was strictly taboo for white people to mix in with Indian religion — let alone burials.

The Eclipse and Indians

To really understand Indians one must also know something of their religion, their belief in the supernatural, and what part the sun and the earth played in their lives.

Nearly every Indian was an implicit believer in dreams. If he had a dream — then that dream ruled his or her life until another dream came along.

Next, nearly every Indian believed that the earth was his or her mother and that the sun was the father. Thus, if an avalanche or earthquake came along — panic was almost epidemic among his people. It meant that mother earth was changing, mad at them, or was being taken by some unseen force.

As important to them was their father — the sun. And, you must remember that there were a high number of eclipses of the sun — partial and total — during the years there were wars between Indians and soldiers, settlers, and pioneers in the West.

So, the total eclipse of the sun not only brought the Henry Draper Eclipse Expedition to the area near Rawlins in 1878, it also excited and panicked a very large number of Indians stretching clear across the Rocky Mountain area.

Draper brought Germans, English, French, Russians, Prussians, Austrians, and Americans, among whom was Tom Edison to Wyoming that year to observe this phenomenon. And, while Samuel P. Langley was pointing his huge telescope at the sun from atop 14,400 feet Pikes Peak — several new Indian messiahs were being created by the total eclipse.

According to reports, listed eclipses of the sun were observed in the West and Wyoming in 1878, 1882, 1884, 1885, 1886, and 1889. I mention those especially because in nearly every case, some new messiah or medicine man with supernatural powers got his strength from an eclipse.

One such was Wovoka, the Piaute whose dream religion finally led the Sioux into the tragedy of Wounded Knee.

Wovoka, who was called Jack Wilson by the white rancher who employed him in Nevada, was sick with a fever in 1878 when the total eclipse of the sun occurred. This blackness at noon caused great excitement in his tribe, but he had already prophesied to his father that the sun would be devoured but would come back — he said he had seen it in a dream!

Thus, when the eclipse did occur, Wovoka proved to his people he had supernatural powers. And, during the eclipse, he dreamed he went to his father who showed him what it was like there and how his people — all Indians — could get back their land, their buffalo, and by use of Ghost Dances and Ghost Shirts painted with mysterious symbols, which could turn a bullet, would at last run the white man off their land.

His father the sun, also gave him control over the elements, and he could make it rain, snow, or be dry — as he wished. Of course, you had to dance for five days for this, he said. But, if you did, everything would be alright.

Wovoka never held a dance when there was no chance of rain, or snow, or heat. No matter, he did have his dream during an eclipse, which he had forecast, and his word was law for twenty years in the West and out of it came the Ghost Dancers who died like flies before the blazing guns of the U.S. Army at Wounded Knee.

He said later on, his father had been mad at him that day. The dreamer religion still carries on today in the West.

Eagle Trapping

I'll bet you did not know that eagle feathers were used as a medium of exchange between Indians on the High Plains and the Rocky Mountains. They were as highly sought after as good ponies and together — ponies and eagle feathers — carried off the day's prize in trading.

Actually, the eagle was regarded as sacred by the Indians out in this region. They used his entire body for various purposes.

Feathers most valued were from the tail and the wing. They were used to ornament lances and shields, to wear upon their heads, and to mount upon their coup sticks. Finally, they were used in making the magnificent head dresses, or war bonnets, the best of which reached from the warrior's head to the ground when he stood fully erect.

In the sun dance, the whistle used by the dancers is the bone from the leg or wing of an eagle. No other bone can be substituted.

Fans carried by the Indians were often made from the entire wing or entire tail of the eagle.

In the early days the war bonnet or fan was the most important part of an Indian's wardrobe and seldom were they traded or bought.

In the East, an eagle could be shot by gun or arrow. In the West, a different situation existed. No one could shoot an eagle. He must be trapped in a pitfall, and then strangled or crushed to death if possible without shedding blood.

Over on the Wind River Reservation the Arapahos live, and this is the manner in which a single man must go out to get his feathers and bones.

The warrior would leave his home for the high country where eagles lived. He would scoop out earth, forming a pit, and carry the dirt a long way from the pit so the eagle would not be wary of the newly dug pit. Then, the warrior would cover the top of the pit with grass and strong sticks and earth. On top of this he would place tallow stripped from buffalo ribs, or a fresh piece of meat. He attached a strong rope of leather to this bait. Then he would sit inside for four days and four nights trying to lure the huge birds to his trap.

He would scare away lesser birds. When an eagle swooped down — always landing a few feet to one side — he would hold his breath waiting for the big bird to hop up on the roof and while the bird was devouring the bait, he would silently reach up through the roof, grasp the bird's legs, drag him down into his pit, and try to strangle the bird or break its neck. Many and many a time, the bird won the battle and the Indian, bearing eagle claw lascerations, would stumble out into the open, rebait his pitfall, and try all over again.

At the end of a four-day period, for he was allowed only four days a year to do this, he would return to his lodge and strip the birds of their feathers and bones, where his wife would then make the fans, war bonnets, and whistles necessary to his manhood, his religion, and his culture.

Wovoka — The Messiah

You cannot help but feel deep sorrow for the proud Indian as you look back over his contact with white man on this continent. He just never had a chance. He was a Stone Age man desperately trying to hold his land, his tribe, his family, and his beliefs fast against the onrushing and everspreading hordes of white men who came from every corner of the world to spill off ships along all coast lines to fill up this huge and bountiful land.

Up to this time, the Indian was the caretaker of the water, the forests, the animals, and the land. And, it seemed to them, that there was enough for everyone.

Occasionally the Indians rose up and joined together in battle to try to stop the awesome steamroller of whites crushing them out of existence. The Pueblo Indians rose up in 1680; Pontiac did it in 1763 in the Great Lakes region; then Tecumsee led his people in the Creek War, and later the Seminoles in Florida.

And, way out here in the West we had our wars, too. We know about them running the gauntlet of fire and blood on the plains between 1850 and 1890 (December 29, 1890, to be exact) when the Wounded Knee Massacre took place.

Each of these wars, uprisings, or series of related battles were invoked by a messiah, a medicine man, or some sort of highly thought of religious leader. Thus, it was out in the Walker River country of Nevada, a young Piaute Indian by the name of Wovoka, son of White Man, or Tavibo, saw a vision and related it to his friends, who passed the word, and out of it came the Wounded Knee fight.

The ancient people were singing:

For the fires grow cold and the dances fail,
And the songs in their echoes die;
And what have we left but the grave beneath
And, above, the waiting sky?

News of the messiah spread from tribe to tribe and from nation to nation. Emissaries traveled by foot, by horse, and even by train to Nevada to visit this Wovoka. He told them of an avalanche that would turn the earth over. It would make the land green with grass, good for the return of the buffalo, and crossed over many times by clear streams. He told them of living in harmony with each other, and that white man would leave them alone.

Over on the Wind River Reservation, the Northern Arapaho sang this song around their fires at night:

My Father, have pity on me!
I have nothing to eat,
I am dying of thirst —
Everything is gone!

And, it was called a Ghost Song and became a part of the Ghost Dance religion that swept the plains. Wovoka told them he was the prophet, he had been invited to heaven several times, described heaven and told them if they went back home and danced and believed — their utopia would arrive.

Some of them became impatient and turned this man's words around into a fighting creed and wearing Ghost shirts with mysterious symbols painted on them, covered with a sacred red paint, and powerful symbols — they fearlessly believed no bullet could kill them.

At Wounded Knee the tragedy of the Ghost Dance was blasted and several hundred Sioux met their death before the blazing guns of the Army. It was to be the last resistance. It tragically signalled the end of Plains wars.

Ten Thousand Indians and Thirty Thousand Horses

Here is a story about Wyoming that has been recorded a number of times, but never with the proper emphasis. It deals with the great peace treaty signed in 1851 at, or near Fort Laramie, between the United States and the High Plains Indians.

Ever since gold fever had swept the nation with the rich California discovery in 1848, emigrants had swarmed across the western plains by the thousands. Bringing their livestock, their wagons, all their earthly goods in one fell swoop — the Indians were, at first, simply thunderstruck and astounded by the number of white-hides.

By 1850, Indians saw the wide scar of destruction the emigrants left in their wake. Buffalo gone along the North Platte, grass gone, disease in the form of cholera sweeping into their tepees and taking their loved ones — it was too much. Something must be done, and they showed their anger in angry gestures, small raids, and defiance of promises made between them and their old friends, the mountain men who were now scouting for the Army and for the long lines of swaying, canvas-covered prairie schooners.

Finally, the government was persuaded to hold a general peace council in September of 1851. Scouts, mountain men, and half-breeds were sent to all points of the compass and told to invite the various tribes in for annuities the government felt they owed the Indians.

At the end of July, Indian tribes began to show up at Fort Laramie. First the Sioux, then their friends the Arapaho and Cheyenne came in to parlay with the white-hides. The army post only had a compliment of around 300 soldiers, and there was general apprehension that when the Crow and Shoshone made their appearance no one was going to be able to hold them from joining in a battle with their deadly enemies among the Sioux, Arapaho, and Cheyenne.

One observer said that when the word arrived that Chief Washakie and his nation were arriving, an aggravated Sioux warrior dashed at them, but before he could get within arrow range a mountain man caught up with him and threw the Sioux warrior to the ground and disarmed him. This act averted, what Jim Bridger later said could have been one of the bloodiest battles ever seen between Indians. You see, Bridger had taken the opportunity to equip the Shoshones with good rifles for their own protection, knowing full well that the Sioux were armed with smooth bore guns and bows and arrows.

In any event, by the end of July it is reckoned that 10,000 Indians from most of the Plains had converged at Fort Laramie, and it was also reckoned that each Indian had, on the average, about three horses.

Imagine if you can a herd of 30,000 horses complete with

10,000 wild Indians gathered on the banks of the Laramie River near Fort Laramie! This scene, never before seen in the annals of American history, was never repeated. All Indians were on their best behavior, dressed in their finest clothing, riding their finest war horses, were led down the North Platte River early in September to a point where Horse Creek flows into the main river. They had to be moved because there simply was not enough grass to keep a herd of horses that size in feed.

As they moved in stately procession thirty-six miles down from the Army post, a mounted military band played martial airs, the Indian Commissioners riding in festooned and colorfully painted carriages and wagons, while another 10,000 dogs — Indian dogs — howled and barked along with each Indian tribe singing its own national songs.

The scene must have been overpowering, and remembering that the thirty-six mile ride took nearly three days, it turned out to be one of the longest parades ever held in the wild, wild, West.

The treaty? Oh, yes. It turned out fine. It was probably the most successful treaty council ever held in the West. But, the sad fact is that it lasted only a couple of years and by 1854, following the Grattan Massacre, battles, campaigns, and skirmishes were fought between red and white men for forty years in the West.

Part Two
Pathfinders and Pioneers

Jim Bridger

If you were to haul off and name ten men who were important to the development of Wyoming, I bet Jim Bridger's name would not be on the list. Maybe, not even on the top twenty.

His is a name in our history we sort of slide over. Yet, between his eighteenth birthday in 1822 and up to the day he died in 1881, "Big Throat" as the Indians called him, left his name along nearly every section of what is now Wyoming.

He first came West with General Ashley's fur trapping expedition, and when he saw the Wind River Mountains, the valley of the Green River, he fell in love with the area. This happened to many a fur trapper.

In and out of the fur trapping business for the next twenty years, Bridger was the man who "helped" to discover Yellowstone Park and also, as far as is known, the first white man to visit and see the Great Salt Lake.

Many is the time that he elaborated upon a true fact to the point where the newcomer to the West, or "Pilgrim" as he was called, could not tell fact from fancy.

For instance, he once told a man who remarked on how beautiful 10,800 foot Laramie Peak was, that when he "fust come out this way, that 'er peak wuz jus' a hole in tha groun!" And when he spent a winter at Fort Laramie visiting with Sir St. George Gore, the Irish nobleman from Sligo who loved talking with the mountain man, Bridger listened with rapture to Gore's reading from Shakespeare.

Bridger was reported to have said about Shakespeare, "Ah reckin'd he was too highfalutin' for me." He went, "Ah rather calcerlated that thar big Dutchman, Mr. Full-stuff, was a lettle too fond of lager beer." Bridger thought, "Twood uv been better for the old man to have stuck to bourbon whiskey straight."

It was said Gore also read to him from Baron Munchausen, the celebrated European liar. When Sir George finished reading about the Baron, Bridger said, "He'd be dog'oned ef he swallered everything that thar Baron Munchausen said." He did acknowledge later on that his own adventures would be nearly as good if put into book form.

According to some authorities, Bridger was the first man to deal in cattle in Wyoming. And, at one time along with his partner Kit Carson, the two skimmed oil from a seep spring on Poison Spider west of Casper, mixed it with flour, and sold it to emigrants along the Oregon Trail as axel grease.

When gold was discovered in Virginia City way up in Montana, Bozeman and Bridger competed to find a good trail from about where Casper is, north into that gold strike area. We know about Bozeman's Trail up the eastern flanks of the Big Horns, but few remember that Bridger blazed a trail from Casper, up into the Big Horn Basin near Worland, and thence into Montana. His trail was never popular because it was too much up and down hill; still, if they had used it, maybe a little less blood would have been spilled in Powder River region on the Bozeman Trail.

One should visit his fort, which he built near Lyman, Wyoming. Wyoming needs to learn more about this man whose name was given to a fort, a forest, an electric plant, a lake, wilderness area, a National Forest, ferry, and a whole slew of commercial ventures.

Father DeSmet

No history of the West or Wyoming is really complete unless the impact of the religious missionaries is described. The biggest share of the mountain men who penetrated what is now Wyoming were skilled in the ways of beaver trapping, could read trail signs as

no one else could, and survived under extreme conditions. But, while they were keen on survival, they were illiterate for the most part. Thus, they welcomed the missionaries from the standpoint of bringing hope and religion to the West, and also, because a missionary was an educated man who could read and write.

Thus, many a missionary earned his way with mountain men by writing letters for them, carrying on educated conversations around camp fires, and by reading various passages from the Bible to them!

Outstanding missionaries who spent time in Wyoming in the early days were Samuel Parker, a Presbyterian minister who came West in 1835 with Dr. Marcus Whitman. Both men visited the Green River Rendezvous that year. Dr. Whitman helped remove an arrowhead from Jim Bridger's back at that rendezvous.

Both men returned in 1836, after visiting the Eastern seaboard, where Whitman was married. A young couple, Henry and Eliza Spalding, and William Gray, another missionary, joined them for the trip West. Thus, white women were brought West first by missionaries.

In fact, the two women spent most of July 1836 at the Rendezvous on the Green River, where both mountain men and Indians were held in awe by their presence. One trapper whooped, "White women! I haven't seen a white woman in twenty years!"

A few years later, Reverend Richard Vaux arrived at Fort Laramie as the post chaplain. He also served as schoolmaster for what was probably the first organized school in Wyoming. Vaux served on the Army post for nearly fifteen years.

The Mormons moved West in 1847 and found a new land in which to live, colonize, and practice their religion without fear of persecution. Their brilliant leader was Brigham Young. His ideas of settling Utah, his organizational qualities, and his zest for the West along with the avid and faithful followers who helped him carry out his work, probably left the greatest impact on the wild western country of any religion or missionary.

Still, for solitary work, for zeal, for getting around all over the West, and for being recognized as a very real authority on the barren plains, the towering mountains and the red men who lived out here, Father "Black Robes" Pierre Jean DeSmet had no equal.

The U.S. government turned to him for his advice and help to organize the greatest peace council ever held in the West at Fort Laramie in 1851. And, Father DeSmet responded by bringing in thirty-five Indian chiefs who otherwise probably would not have attended the council. It is interesting to note here that while the treaty was going on, Father DeSmet was busy, too. He remarked in his diary in September 1851, that he baptized 955 Arapaho, Cheyenne, Brule, and Oglala Sioux children! That he had a dry sense of humor is also evident at this same time when he explained that due to lack of enough beef to go around to the 10,000 Indians at the Fort Laramie meeting, many feasts whose main fare was dog meat were held. DeSmet said, "The feasts were numerous and well attended. No epoch in Indian annals, probably, shows a greater massacre of the canine race."

Coming West in 1840, Father DeSmet, a Jesuit priest who had come from Belgium, entered his field of labor as a missionary to the Indians. His advice, not only to Indian agents, Army officers, emigrants, but to the Indians was well heeded. In fact, it was Father DeSmet who told the Sioux about the worth of the gold in the Black Hills, and told them not to let white man enter, or there would be much trouble. The Indians listened, but white man could not stay away, a fact that helped lead to the annihilation of Colonel George Armstrong Custer's entire command in 1876.

In August 1851, as Father DeSmet was making his way from the Yellowstone region to Fort Laramie to attend the great council, he wrote: (August 24) "We arrived quite unexpectedly on the borders of a lovely little lake about six miles long, and my traveling companions gave it my name." Thus, Lake DeSmet was given a name, and if you stop off to visit the lake between Buffalo and Sheridan, Wyoming, take your fishing rod with you, because, Lake DeSmet is well known for its fighting rainbow trout as well as its historic significance.

The Second White Man Into Wyoming

Searching for the shores of the Western Seas brought the de la Verendrye brothers and two other Frenchmen into Wyoming in 1743. These men, the first white men to penetrate into what we now call Wyoming, came in 1742 through the Dakotas, and probably wound up after encountering the "Gens des Serpent," Snake Indians, in January 1743 somewhere in the vicinity of Gillette.

Pierre de la Verendrye was the Chevalier, a lower order of nobility, who led the party into Wyoming. His brother, Francois, came with him.

That was twenty years prior to the American Revolution. And these two men, following in the footsteps of their father who had searched clear across the Eastern half of Canada for a route West, drew to a halt when they encountered the "Gens des Serpents," as they noted in their historic log.

Two other Frenchmen accompanied these two intrepid explorers. They were Edouard la Londette and Jean Baptiste Amoitte.

All four left their names carved on a metal plate unearthed many years later at Pierre, South Dakota. Hence, we know they went on West, or I should say, that they had been West, and when they buried the plate in their King's name, the Sun King, it was on their return trip.

A long, long time would pass before the second recorded white man came into Wyoming. Perhaps at some future date, and still resting in some forgotten journal, a diary will show logged penetration into Wyoming. But, until that journal is found, then the next recorded trip to Wyoming came sixty-two years later, or in 1805 to be precise.

At that time Francois Antoine Larocque wrote in his journal that he had left roughly the same area around where Bismarck is today, and that he knew of Lewis and Clark, who wintered where Bismarck is, in 1804.

Larocque entered the region north of Gillette from the Little Missouri River in July 1805. He called the Powder River by its right name — Chakadee Wakoa — a Crow name meaning powdery stream.

Larocque called the prickly pear cactus the "Crone de Racquette." He wrote about the dry plains and chalk cliffs. He talked about the elk-deer, presumably elk. He discussed the jumping deer, probably the mule deer bounding off in their coiled spring-like movements. He called the antelope, cabrio. And, he discussed the buffalo as the horned animals.

One thing he cautiously mentioned was the bad tempered yellow and white bear that he said were very fierce. He was, of course, showing he had met a grizzly bear or two, and lost the battle of right-of-way with the huge monster that owned that part of the West in those days.

While Larocque was there, High Plains Indians were engaged in a contest for the great Powder River Basin, which was to be the literal cockpit of warfare between not only Crow and Sioux with their allies, the Northern Arapaho and the Northern Cheyenne; but, also the very bloody struggle that was to last forty years between elements of the U.S. Army, and the Red Army of the West commanded by various Indian chiefs, not the least of whom was Red Cloud.

Whatever the case may have been in the 1860s, the de la Verendrye brothers saw and described the "shining mountains" reckoned by most historians as the towering Big Horns, well over 120 years before General Connor led his forces into the Sioux sanctuary of the Powder River in the summer of 1865.

We also know the second white man to come into the area in the summer of 1805 was Francois Antoine Larocque, two years after the Louisiana Purchase was made, and a good six years before Wilson Price Hunt led the overland Astorians past Gillette in 1811.

Bridger's Road

It is conceivable that had the road Jim Bridger blazed to Virginia City, Montana Territory, in 1864 become more popular than the so-called Bozeman Trail, much bloodshed and even the Custer Massacre might have been avoided.

While it is not generally known, Jim Bridger really did open a trail, or road, along the western flanks of the Big Horn Mountains in the summer of 1864, through the Big Horn Basin.

Gold had been discovered in 1862 in Virginia City, Montana Territory, and this glittering magnet drew, as it always did, hordes of miners and emigrants west, and into that region of the Rockies.

One way to get to Virginia City was up the Missouri River to Fort Benton, then on the third road to the gold fields — the Mullen Road — south to Helena and then into the Bozeman region to Virginia City.

Another way was the trail John Bozeman and John Jacobs planned and promoted. It would save 400 miles to the newly discovered goldfields. That is, if you stayed on the Emigrant Trail, or Oregon Trail, and then turned north at La Bonte Creek into the Powder River country to the Yellowstone River. There you turned west and just followed your nose to Virginia City.

Only one trouble with the Montana Trail, or Bozeman Trail. The Indians did not like it. They felt the Powder River Basin belonged to them; they had signed treaties to keep it for their hunting grounds, and were really apprehensive that white-hides, as they called the white men, would soon take over their sacred hunting grounds. They were right in the long run.

In between, hundreds of men, women, and children, both white and red, were to lose their lives from Casper north to Montana because Bozeman turned out to be a better promoter than Bridger.

That's about the size of it. Jim Bridger had years and years of plains and mountain experience behind him. He knew he would have no trouble leaving Casper at about the Red Buttes, heading north over the southern end of the Big Horn Mountains, and coming out into the Big Horn Basin just above Thermopolis. Then, he would follow the Big Horn up past Worland, Greybull, and past the Stinking Water River, now called the Shoshone, near Cody before striking the friendly Yellowstone and a calm trip to Virginia City.

Besides, Bridger was a great and true friend of Chief Washakie. Washakie and the Shoshone Indians more or less controlled the Big Horn Basin area, and when Bridger did meet with Washakie in the summer of 1864, he got the green light.

Still, Bozeman and his partner, Jacobs, who really lead the way, outsold Bridger. So, battles familiar to the ear — Hayfield fight, Wagon Box, Fetterman Massacre, as well as the Custer Massacre — became part of the tragic aftermath of one road being overpromoted.

Those living then should have followed Bridger — not Bozeman.

The Pony Express

On January 27, 1860, W.H. Russell telegraphed Washington, D.C., "Have determined to establish a Pony Express to Sacramento, California commencing the 3rd of April. Time — ten days." This was good news to Washington, because up to then it took twenty-five to thirty days to get news from one coast to another, and with the nation on the brink of Civil War, news of the West was vital.

Russell, often called the father of the Pony Express, sent out word to buy 500 head of horses and asked his partner, Alexander Majors, to supervise the hiring of nearly one hundred good riders and two hundred more steady men to man the way stations between St. Joe, Missouri, and Sacramento, California.

Now that over one hundred years have passed since the creation of this "ride for time," few people realize that the Pony Express only lasted eighteen months before it was made obsolete with the creation of the telegraph lines stretching across the nation. Yet, during that time when an ounce of mail cost $10 to carry, the Pony Express was the only really fast communication link in our country.

So, men like Bill Cody, Pony Bob Haslam, and Jim Moore — all three top notch express riders — helped to bind a nation together. Business news between the coasts was important, news of friends, relatives, and loved ones was dear, and government dispatches were critical and crucial. The riders, often ambushed by Indians and road agents, fighting swirling dust storms, galloping across blistering hot plains, and through icy blizzards kept their schedule with amazing accuracy and certainly, heart, courage, and tenacity.

Jim Moore could well lay claim to one of the hardest rides in history. Leaving Midway Station in the western part of Nebraska, he rode to Julesburg, Colorado. As he rode in, a very important government dispatch arrived at the same time. With no rider available, Moore turned around and carried the dispatch back to Midway Station. He made the round trip in fourteen hours and forty-six minutes, all the while riding at a gallop a distance of 280 miles!

Bill Cody rode the division between Red Buttes (near Casper) on the North Platte River and the Three Crossings on the Sweetwater. And, Pony Bob Haslam one time rode 190 miles, finding at each station the relief rider either dead or wounded, which meant he had to keep right on riding until he found a relief rider ready to go.

It was not often that a rider had to pack more than ten pounds of mail at one clip. And, his ride usually ran from sixty-five to one hundred miles on his division with three to four way stations located within the division. At each station, the rider was allowed two minutes to dismount, grab his mail bags, jump on a fresh horse, and ride off.

The big test was the winter ride, but the intrepid riders made twenty-two midwinter trips over the Rockies and Sierras averaging 13.8 days, while only missing one trip. Thus, the semiweekly mail service proved itself to the satisfaction of all including the government that passed an act providing for a daily mail and semiweekly mail. The Pony Express was finally displaced by the telegraph on October 24, 1861.

Yet, the growth of the West saw these lithe, courageous riders help bind one coast to another during the eighteen months that the Pony Express existed, and the indelible mark left by the riders on the pages of our history is still identified by the sign on our special delivery letters today — a speeding horseman on a galloping horse carrying the mail.

The Powder River Trail

Once the Great Treaty Council of 1851 was concluded, Indians who had been a part of the huge meeting were to be allowed an annual annuity amounting to $50,000 worth of trade goods, beef, and other items for the next ten years.

It was a good treaty insofar as the Sioux, the Arapaho, and the Cheyenne were concerned. All they had to do was to come to an area designated near Fort Laramie, and divide the loot.

For any other Indians, it became a nearly impossible feat to find a neutral place at which their fair share of the annuities could be given them.

Remember, the Crow had fought and lost the Powder River region to the Sioux and their allies, the Northern Arapaho and Northern Cheyenne. The Crow were blood enemies of those three Indian nations, and there was continual warfare between them for years and years. That is one reason why the Crow worked for the white soldiers — the "walk-aheaps" — as they called the infantry, and the "yellow-legs" as they called the cavalry. They would do anything to help the white-hide soldiers defeat the Sioux, Arapaho, and Cheyenne.

But that did not solve how they were to receive their spoils from the Treaty of 1851.

In 1836, Captain Bonneville had sent a Portuguese to build a trading post on the forks of the Powder River. This fur trading post was called simply "The Portuguese Houses." Jim Bridger mentioned the fact he and a number of his fur trapping brothers had spent several weeks there, and that they had held off a war party of Sioux for several weeks. It was also mentioned that Bridger and his brigade of men had practically eaten the Portuguese, Antonio Matero, out of house and home and supplies.

Twenty-three years later, Jim Bridger led a U.S. Topographical Engineering party to the ruins of the Portuguese Houses in the fall of 1859. Captain W.F. Raynolds noted the old buildings in his official journals and even went so far as to use an ax edge to shave off one of the smooth logs so he could write a message for a brother engineering officer who saw it a few days later. That would be Lieutenant H.E. Maynadier.

Raynolds said that he had met a Spaniard there at the old fur trading post. Raynolds had been expecting to meet the Spaniard there because all the way south from the Yellowstone, Raynolds and his party had attracted a large number of Crow who followed his little column of "bugg ketchers" and other scientists with them. These Crow, as it turned out, were on their way to meet the Spaniard, and there at the Portuguese Houses, they would receive their share of the annuities of the Treaty of 1851.

It seems that the Commissioners knew the Crow had little chance of sliding south to Fort Laramie through the Sioux-Arapaho-Cheyenne infested country to get their annuities. So, Joseph Bissonette, an American Fur Company trader, was hauling them from Fort Laramie to about where Casper is today, and then heading north on the little known "Powder River Trail" to make the delivery to the Crow.

Raynolds mentioned the little-known trail in his logged journal, but so far as Wyoming history and historians are concerned, little has ever been written or said about the trail which fed the Crow, and helped keep them off the warpath for a number of years.

Cholera

It was tough enough, driving a yoke of oxen two thousand miles from St. Louis to California over the Oregon Trail, let alone fighting cholera, too. But, sad as it was, cholera was epidemic in the United States in 1849, and one of its grave-strewn trails led right through Wyoming as evidenced by the headstones — wood and stone — marking the way West.

Cholera, passed from man to man and by food, by touch, through drinking contaminated water, and other forms of pollution, caused at the lowest estimate nearly five thousand deaths along the Oregon Trail. I have no record of what happened on the sister trail south — the Santa Fe Trail — but my guess is that it was equally bad.

According to the best information I can find, cholera in 1849 hit St. Louis in April of that year. By the end of June , five thousand two hundred eighty-five deaths had occurred in that city alone.

We all know that St. Louis and the small towns around it were the terminals for getting outfitted for the long and hazardous journey to the glory holes and gold littered sandbars along the Sacramento River in California, where gold had been discovered. It is reasonable to figure then, with cholera rampant in St. Louis, that emigrants passing through would pick it up and carry it West with them. And, this is just exactly what happened.

Cholera played no favorites, and it struck with lightning-like force. For instance, Major Cross, quartermaster for the Regiment of Mounted Riflemen, said his top wagonmaster died within several hours about where the Hat Six Ranch would be located near Casper, Wyoming, today. They had been riding after several buffalo in the region when Sam Miller, his wagonmaster, said he felt badly. Returning to camp on the North Platte, the Major said Miller was seized by cholera and died within several hours. The date was July 1, 1849.

An Englishman, the Honorable Henry J. Coke, the grandson of the famed English lawyer Richard Coke, said that many of the emigrants died because of ignorance, uncleanliness, and general change in diet. He had hit near the truth, and none of his party visiting America were taken by the dreaded illness; no doubt because they took lots of medicine, boiled their water, and kept to a diet of well-cooked food.

Coke said, "I for one have swallowed nearly an apothecary's shop full of paregoric, opium pills and cholera powders." He had, in fact, a drugstore with him. One thing for sure, he went to California and in good health.

Health seemed to improve west of Fort Laramie; better drinking water is one guess. Yet, if the emigrants would have taken their water from the North Platte — brown and dirty as it looked — many hundreds of them would have survived, instead of drinking from the clear, cool, deadly pools of contaminated water along the Oregon Trail as it crossed Nebraska and into Wyoming.

Part Three
The Army

Thanksgiving at Fort McKinney

Away from the social swirl of the Eastern seaboard, and the bright lights of St. Louis, New Orleans, and Chicago, the Army and its friends — the ranchers and townsmen — really laid it on when it came to celebrating a holiday.

I have in mind Thanksgiving Day, 1882, at Fort McKinney near Buffalo, Wyoming.

Preparations began as early as the fifteenth of October when a wagon was sent all the way to Cheyenne — a distance of well over four hundred miles — round trip, and brought back with it fruit, oysters, eggs, candies, nuts, and other treats for the big occasion. Troop "I" of the Fifth Cavalry and the post commandant, Colonel Kellogg, contributed $60 from troop funds.

This amount went into the "extras" for the celebration.

Add to it a dozen fine mule deer, a number of antelope, a couple of elk and buffalo, sage chicken, rabbits, and crisp celery, early potatoes and pumpkin from the post garden, and you begin to see what was going to happen when Thanksgiving Day arrived.

Invitations, printed on fine paper imported from Wisconsin, were sent out, and as each honored guest and his family arrived and entered the gaily decorated barracks, a soldier in full dress uniform met them at the door, saluted them gracefully, and took charge of their traveling attire. The soldier then announced them to all assembled who had already arrived.

The chandelier was twenty unsheathed sabers hanging downward, their reflection casting bright lantern light dancing all round the room. Flags were draped along the walls, mottos beneath them, and bouquets in flower pots sending their fragrance were scattered throughout the hall. The music of the post band helped bring back fond and nostalgic memories to many a man and woman hundreds of miles from their original homes.

The total attendance at this social extravaganza of the season was over 300, and after going through the opening grand march they danced at their very own ball until midnight.

Then they sat down to eat. Each table was decorated with a guardhouse made of corned beef with a carrot carved into a sentry with a rifle in his hands. A large, three-foot high cake stood on each table, covered with flags like a castle, and across the end of the hall, in evergreens this motto, "Let good digestion wit no appetite, and health on both!"

Outside, grinning Cheyenne and Crow Indians pressed against the glass windows observing white-hides and their women dancing the light fantastic, and whooping it up.

The menu for the evening or midnight meal was mock turtle soup, roast pork, elk and buffalo roast, smoked antelope, venison roast, sage chicken, corned beef, boiled ham, chicken, potato salad, assorted pickles, tomato sauce, Worchestershire sauce, pumpkin pie, floating island, fruit cakes, gold and marble cakes, apples, oranges, chocolate and jelly cakes, candies, coffee and tea.

At 5:00 A.M., they stopped dancing long enough to consume a huge breakfast, hitch up their wagons, saddle their horses, and ride back to their respective homes. This was the big social event of the season. It was too cold and tough to do it on Christmas or New Year's, and I suspect that after a party like that it was enough to carry them through the bitter winter months until "green grass" time in April.

Custard — Not Custer!

You know, one of the battles overlooked in the winning of the West was the battle Sergeant Custard — not Custer — fought a few miles west of Fort Caspar on the old telegraph road.

Not taking anything away from the gallant young Lieutenant Caspar Collins, who lost his life on the same day — July 26, 1865 — but those who live in the Casper area in their rush to explain how Casper got its name have really never given enough thought, research, nor examination of Commissary Sergeant Amos J. Custard who, along with twenty-five men fought a terrible battle against overwhelming odds of Sioux, Cheyenne, and Arapaho Indians just a few miles west from, and in sight of, Platte Bridge, now called Fort Caspar, on July 26, 1865.

I really do not think many people realize that young Caspar Collins was one of six killed that morning. He alone did not perish. Five other good men were killed, too.

That afternoon, Sergeant Custard and nineteen others were horribly tortured, mutilated, and then scalped four miles upstream from the Platte River Bridge. And, just prior to that, three men survived to gain their lives at the post, out of a detachment Custard had sent of six men to reconnoiter the area ahead of their wagon train.

So, all in all, July 26, 1865, was a very bloody day near Casper, what with twenty-six soldiers being killed and three civilian teamsters being killed. No one knows how many Indians were killed, but evidence left behind indicates they had more killed than they were able to kill. The day-long battle must have taken upwards of one hundred men — red and white.

There is not time here to go into all the details of the actual battle Custard had. Suffice to say, after he had sent out a scouting party of six men, three of whom were to die before they got to the Platte River Bridge, his supply train was surrounded by a howling horde of Indians bent upon vengeance.

Some say that the vengeance the Indians were after was a random shot some fool fired a few weeks earlier at a young Indian boy riding across the bridge to see an Indian girl encamped with her family near the post. The boy was killed. It is said that the boy was the son of a war chief of the Cheyenne.

This caused the battle, not only of Platte River Bridge, but also the Custard Wagon fight.

One wonders, looking over the various records and, believe me, the varying and confusing tales about the men who were at the post, why they never went to the rescue of Custard. They could see the wagon tops of Custard's beleaguered outfit. They could hear the shots. They could see the swarming Indians, and they had a command of nearly two hundred men. But they did not send a relief to Custard.

The excuse that is offered, as one goes back through the records, was that they did not have enough ammunition; that the post was not to be lost; that their duties did not permit them to leave the post.

Whatever the reason, in the records of the annals of Plains warfare, July 26, 1865, at and near Casper, Wyoming, was a very bloody day.

Ambulance

Does the word ambulance bring certain pictures to your mind? It sure does to me. I think of flashing lights, sirens, and somebody in trouble.

But, if you read diaries and various phases of early western history, you will find the same word creating a different set of impressions — certainly not an ambulance full of groaning men full of wounds or arrows being taken to a hospital.

The ambulance of the sixties and seventies was designed to carry the wounded. Sure enough. But, it found itself being used mainly as an Army stagecoach more than being used as an "Ammbuulaancee!" (That is how old-time Army people pronounced it.)

When an officer together with his wife and family, or a married enlisted man or noncommissioned officer was transferred from one post to another, the best means of moving him if there was no railroad handy, was by using the four-mule team driven ambulance.

One lady, a Mrs. Burt who was stationed at Fort Bridger in 1866, at Fort Sanders in 1867, at Fort Kearney in 1868, and at Fort C.F. Smith the same year before moving to Fort D.A. Russell, which was located near Cheyenne, was moved on all occasions in an ambulance.

She wrote in her diary that she had a milk cow named Bessie, and that the cow learned to travel along right behind the ambulance. On the back of the wagon she had an old red rooster and a dozen hens in a wicker basket tied and these birds, too, traveled with her and her growing family from post to post.

Up near where old Fort Reno was once located about half way between Casper and Gillette now, she was riding along in her ambulance where an angry war party of Sioux attacked them. She

got down behind the side boards, hid her two children, a boy about six and a brand new baby girl only three months old, and kept her head down while the cavalry escort fought off the savage raid. Two men were killed, and three were injured, but Mrs. Burt and her family came through without a scratch, just some splinters that she got from trying to keep flat on the wooden floor of the ambulance.

The ambulance was also used to carry inspectors of the Army as they traveled back and forth from post to post. It was also used to carry the payroll from post to post. And, many an ambulance was used by a soldier and his family and their friends to take a picnic in, or to go on sage chicken hunting expeditions.

So, the ambulance we think of today and the ambulance that traveled in Wyoming a hundred years ago were really two entirely different types of transportation. We view ours with alarm. They viewed theirs as a vehicle to travel in, to use on picnics, or watched it as it drove into sight carrying a payroll. And they called it an "Amm-buu-laancee!"

Long Service at Fort Laramie

One fellow who has not received much publicity in Wyoming military history sure left his mark at Fort Laramie. This would be a young Swiss by the name of Leodegar Schnyder.

Born in Sursee, Switzerland, in 1814, just about the time America was taming the British in New Orleans, young Schnyder came to the United States with his family to Pittsburg, Pennsylvania, in 1829. At the age of twenty-three he joined the Army. The year was 1837.

He fought against the Seminoles in Florida, served in Florida, the Cherokee Nation, and Missouri. His company was left behind while the rest of his regiment, the Sixth Infantry, went to fight in Mexico in the War of 1846.

In 1849, when Fort Laramie became a military post, Schnyder and his company were transferred to the post. And for the next thirty-seven years, Schnyder was stationed at Fort Laramie. He served longer at that post than any other man.

Being a bookbinder by trade, Schnyder was appointed assistant librarian of the post library in 1851. By 1852, the Swiss had become first sergeant of his company and applied for the position of ordinance sergeant — a position the Army held in high regard.

He got the job, which meant that he was responsible for the good working order of rifles, hand guns, field pieces, ammunition for them, and tools and supplies necessary for their care.

He married in 1852 and had two daughters. But, the first wife died in 1862, and he married again, this time three more daughters were added to his family.

You may ask — why even discuss Schnyder? Well, think of one man serving continuously for thirty-seven years at Fort Laramie. Think of it in terms of the post being an adobe fort when he came, and in 1886, when he left, a big Army post that had seen the Grattan Massacre, thousands of emigrants pass by it, treaties made — and broken — in the shadow of the old post, the Civil War, trouble along the trails passing it with Indians, and the resulting wars with the Indians. Sergeant Schnyder was a witness to all of it.

He even shot a man and killed his horse during the Civil War when the man fired on the Stars and Stripes. He fought up and down the trails above and below the post. He saw, if you will, the passing American parade as the United States grew and grew from thirty-one stars in the flag, while he was at Fort Laramie, to forty stars in the field of blue.

One man wrote, "He lived by a code. He was a man of tested courage and balanced judgement. He was a good soldier."

I guess if someone can say that about you when it is all said and done, then you have done your duty and rate a chapter in not only the history of your country — but Wyoming, too.

WACS In Wyoming

Strange as it may seem, the women of Wyoming notched a first in the liberation movement in getting the vote, by sitting on juries, and one thing I bet many did not know: by serving in the Army before the twentieth century was ushered in.

It's a fact. In Cheyenne, two companies of women were mustered into the United States Army in 1890. Yes, Sir! They had a captain, Emma O'Brien, several lieutenants: Helen Furness, Gertrude Morgan, and Kate Kelly. Emma Schilling was first sergeant, and Adah Haygood was second sergeant.

They were divided into "H" Company and "K" Company. They were drilled by several officers at Fort D.A. Russell, now Warren Air Base.

You may ask what their purpose was? Simple. They were first, the guard of honor at the Wyoming Statehood celebration, and in the second place, the were Guard of Honor to the State Flag.

Yes, Company H was the Guard of Honor of the State float, a very large float, which had a number of younger girls on it, dressed in red, white, and blue, each representing a different State in the

Union. That is — except Idaho and Wyoming, which were just being admitted to the Union at that time.

Company H had to drill for two months, once they were actually sworn into the United States Army. Company K, on the other hand, was the Guard of Honor for the Wyoming State Flag. And, they proudly marched in the big parade in the newly formed state that was the first in the Union to give women the vote. They were the guard for their dearly beloved state ensign.

Oh, yes! They were real enough uniforms, too. Sort of a helmet, popular during the times, later on to be called a "Kaiser Wilhelm" spiked helmet; they carried regulation Army issue rifles with slings; and they had black broadcloth uniforms with long flowing skirts and across the front, gold cord was draped in three rows. They also wore white gloves.

Following the celebration, which took place in Cheyenne, the Girl Guards — as they were called — were disbanded. Still, it would be wise to remember the fact that Wyoming had a Girl Guard unit composed of two companies long before women started their "lib movement" in the second half of the twentieth century, proving once again Wyoming has always believed in equality for both men and women.

U.S.
U.S.

Crook's Jackass Army

Pointing north from Fort Fetterman in May, 1876, Brigadier General George Crooke led five companies of infantry and fifteen troops of cavalry into the Powder River section of Wyoming on the prowl for hostile Indians who had wandered off their reservations in the Dakotas.

Arriving at the site of old Fort Phil Kearny in June, Crook went into bivouac until his Shoshone and Crow Indian scouts could locate the hostile and renegade Indians. Following several days of waiting, his scouts located the enemy a few miles north.

Looking over his command, Crook knew he could never hope to catch mounted Indians with a fourth of his troops on foot. Yet, he could not leave the "walk-a-heaps," as the Indians called the foot soldiers, behind. He reasoned that superior Indian forces might engulf them and wipe them out. So, the wily Indian fighter ordered Major Chambers, the commanding officer of the infantry, to mount his soldiers on the best pack mules available.

The major argued that his soldiers could keep up, that they had not riden mules before, and even more important, the mules had not been ridden either! But the general was adamant, and a reluctant order was finally given to the foot soldiers. Then the fun began as each soldier began his private and individual combat with his long-eared adversary.

Now, Missouri mules are noted for their stubborness. A Missouri mule that had been trained as a pack animal fought for his very life rather than let a soldier throw a McClellan saddle on his back for a leisurely ride across the prairie.

So, the mule employed all the fighting tactics at his command: he bit, he kicked, he brayed, he bucked, ran, fell down, sat down, and in general caused more confusion than a Kansas cyclone. The air was alive with angry shouts and curses, screams of pain and anger; and the "yellow legs" (that's what the Indians called the cavalry soldiers) rode over to shout encouragements and laugh at the spectacle. One observer said many years later that this was probably the largest and most disorganized rodeo event in the whole history of the West!

Looking back, one foot soldier said that after he had finally caught his mule and saddled the "blame brute" as he called it, he tried to ford the Goose Creek. With the banks overflowing with the spring runoff, Goose Creek was high and muddy. The soldier said his mule eased into the water, deeper and deeper and any minute he expected the mule to start swimming. But no, the mule tippy-toed across the stream with only his eyes, ears and nostrils above water and the soldier nearly drowned as he clutched the saddle while the mule gingerly inched across the raging torrent!

After a long march that day, the cavalry pulled into a bivouac area, formed a rectangle and saved one side of the pickett lines for what was now called "Crook's Jackass Army." Major Chambers, doing his best to preserve his dignity and that of the infantry, tried to manuever his troops into the pickett line in a military fashion. But, the mules, seeing the horses tied up and being tired with the extra effort they had put forth that day, sat down and started braying.

It was too much for Chambers. He threw down his saber and tried to resign his commission on the spot. Of course, the offer was refused, and before the Crook's expedition had finished their tour in the field, the mules and soldiers got used to each other and Chambers came to glory in the title given to his command as "Crook's Jackass Army."

The Ghost of Fort Laramie

There are all sorts of ghost stories, but the best one I ever heard was told to me while I was serving as a ranger-historian at Fort Laramie many years ago. I do not know if it is true, but it is such a good story that I want to pass it along.

Here's how it goes. . . . A young officer, recently graduated from West Point, was ordered to his first station, Fort Laramie, Wyoming Territory, in the 1870s. Arriving at Cheyenne, he rode his private Kentucky mount across the plains to the post. After being assigned quarters and duties, he turned his attention to other activities.

Young officers, while stationed at the fort, liked to chase coyotes with a pack of hounds. So, one fine autumn morning, our young officer, along with three new friends, rode southeast over the rolling hills in search of the wily coyote.

After several good chases, the young officer's Kentucky bred horse came up lame. Dismounting, he found the horse was stone bruised. The rocky hills of Wyoming were too much for the horse, until properly shod. It was late afternoon, but only a few miles from the fort, so the young man told his friends he would walk his horse back to the post rather than take a chance of cruelly laming the horse forever.

Moving down a small ravine and on a good trail, he suddenly heard the sound of pounding hoofs in the twilight behind him. Turning, he saw a black stallion bearing directly at him and carrying a woman riding sidesaddle. A second glance assured him that the horse was a runaway. Its nostrils were distended, he could see the whites of the horse's eyes, and it appeared that the foam covered stallion had the bit between his teeth.

Almost involuntarily he made a leap at the bridle, trying to stop the black beast as it tore past him. But the rider raised a riding crop and slashed him on the cheek, throwing him off stride as the horse raced on past him and down the trail out of sight.

Coming to his knees, his mind's eye seemed to capture the picture of a jeweled handle on the riding crop, which caught the dying rays of sunshine as it came down upon his cheek. And, his eyes had caught a fleeting look at a woman dressed in what seemed like a green velvet riding habit, her face and eyes covered by what seemed a lacy black veil.

Then he heard laughter, and looking up, saw his three friends lounging in their saddles on a hill above him. They had seen the whole affair, and kidded him as they rode down, saying he was not much of a horseman when he could not stop a runaway carrying a helpless woman to oblivion.

Yet, when all four mounted their horses and tried to pick up the trail of the black horse, they found no hoofprints in the trail — above or below the scene of action. That night, at the risk of being kidded, the young officer told his story over cigars after dinner. The commanding officer of the post, Colonel Henry C. Merriam said, "Don't laugh at him, for he has just seen the ghost of Fort Laramie!"

The colonel told how a fur factor of the post had brought his high-strung daughter to spend the summer and fall with him at the fort when it was a fur trading fort. The fur trader brought the girl all the way from St. Louis, as he did not want her to run off and marry the man she loved. After arriving at the fort, the trader told his men that she could not leave the fort unless he accompanied her. He sort of held her captive. But one day, she jumped on her own black horse, and rode through the gates at a gallop and was never seen since that day in 1848.

The old colonel paused, and said, "She is seen every seven years. And, this is the seventh year — so you did see the ghost."

Intrigued by the whole affair, the young officer found an interpreter and after visiting Indian lodges around the post found an ancient old squaw who told him she had heard the story, too.

"Yes," she said through the interpreter, "I remember the girl who rode her horse falling off!"

That meant riding sidesaddle.

"She had a green blanket around her and hid her eyes," the squaw said.

That meant the green velvet riding habit and the veil.

Now — the big question.

He asked, "Was she carrying anything in her hand?"

"Yes. She waved a short stick with fire in the handle!"

Satisfied that he had really seen the ghost of Fort Laramie, he still wondered if it was a ghost as he fingered the livid slash across the side of his face!

The Fetterman Disaster

On a bitter cold day in December 1866, Brevet Lieutenant Colonel W.J. Fetterman led his command of eighty-three soldiers out of the stockade surrounding Fort Phil Kearny in relief of a wood cutting detail then under attack from a band of hostile Indians. Earlier that same month, Fetterman had been led into an ambush by Sioux Chief Red Cloud and his fierce warriors, but had been saved by the timely arrival of help from his commanding officer, Colonel Henry Carrington and his hard-riding soldiers.

Colonel Carrington had learned his lesson, but Fetterman later boasted that if he had eighty men, he could ride clean through Red Cloud's dog soldiers.

The stage was set on December 21, 1866. Red Cloud let Fetterman relieve the wood detail, and even though Colonel Carrington had told Fetterman to return to the fort as soon as he got the wood detail out of danger, Fetterman thought he saw a chance to make his boast come true. Red Cloud's men slyly moved just out

of range, yet still presented a challenge to Fetterman. And, as the Indians seemed to retreat, they drew Fetterman further and further away — first over one hill, then another, until Fetterman and his men were safely in Red Cloud's trap. Then, with one huge and massive charge, hundreds of the Sioux leader's warriors simply overran Fetterman and slaughtered the entired command — eighty-three in all — three more than the eighty Fetterman had boasted he would lead to glory.

Events leading up to the fight are important to the story, too. Gold, the glittering magnet that drew men irresistibly toward danger had been discovered in Virginia City, Montana. With the main trail to the West south of the goldfields, many a miner picked his way north from the Oregon Trail straight through treaty territory proclaimed by the government as off limits to white men, while a hunting and living sanctuary for red men.

After numerous attempts to quell the trouble in this area,

which was the Powder River and Tongue River country in Wyoming, the government asked the Indians to come to Fort Laramie to sign another peace treaty.

Even while the treaty was going on, Colonel Carrington and his command arrived with orders to build a string of forts in the Powder River and Tongue River country to protect the miners and emigrants. John Bozeman and Jim Bridger had been hired by the government to find a good trail to Virginia City earlier. Bridger's trail left Fort Laramie, moved through what is now Casper, over to the tail end of the Big Horns, and into the Big Horn Basin before finally winding up in Montana. Bozeman had skirted the edge of the Big Horns on their eastern flanks and found good passage up the length of this range of mountains north into the Yellowstone River region, before he turned West to the Virginia City goldfields.

Bozeman's trail was selected since the trail Bridger blazed was simply too tough to navigate. The only trouble with the Bozeman Trail was the Indians, and Red Cloud hated it and waged a deadly war against those who used it.

Thus, during the summer of 1866 when Colonel Carrington erected Fort Reno, Fort Kearny, and Fort C.F. Smith, he and his men, as well as the miners and others traveling up the trail, were under constant attack. It follows that the Fetterman Massacre was almost inevitable.

After Fetterman and his entire command had been slaughtered, near panic descended upon Fort Kearny. John "Portugee" Phillips, a scout and trader, volunteered to ride to Fort Laramie for help. That night, aboard Colonel Carrington's Kentucky thoroughbred horse, Phillips slipped past the water gap in the stockade walls and for four days and nights braved the danger of being killed by Indians or freezing in the subzero temperatures to bring the message of the disaster to Fort Laramie, a distance of 237 miles. Phillips arrived at Fort Laramie on Christmas night, and a relief expedition was soon on its way. The ride is considered as one of the most courageous in history.

The Wagon Box Victory

Red Cloud divided his army of Sioux, Arapaho, and Cheyenne warriors and leveled twin attacks against Fort C.F. Smith and Fort Phil Kearny on the first and second of August 1867. Both forts guarded the Bozeman Trail, and as such, were intense objects of hatred by the Indians.

Red Cloud reasoned that having whipped Fetterman and over eighty men the previous winter, he could stop the soldiers at both forts from receiving support if he attacked them at the same time. So, splitting his huge war party into two forces, he sent several thousand against the defenders at Fort Smith, August 1, and slipped 100 miles south where he personally led the attack at Fort Kearny.

First, Red Cloud sent his fighting men against a small, wood detail about six miles from Kearny. He noted that a number of wagon boxes were strung out in a semicircle, but that did not stop him, nor his men as they began their fight early on the morning of August 2. None of his warriors felt it would be a hard fight. Instead, the wood detail would give the warriors a taste of what was ahead.

With the first warning shots fired upon them, the soldiers guarding the wood cutters fell back inside of the empty wagon boxes, which were corraled at a strategic position easy to defend. Captain James Powell was in command. He was an officer that had risen from the ranks during the Civil War, and was a seasoned and steady soldier. It was he that had turned the wagon boxes over, and contrary to rumor, these boxes did not have straps of iron plate bolted to them, which would turn angry bullets.

Powell had several things going for him and his men. First, they had just been issued new Springfield breech loading fifty caliber rifles. This rifle was more accurate, could be fired faster, and was to be a surprise to attacking Indians. Powell knew the Indians were counting on the soldiers firing one round, then having to stop to use a ramrod.

While this loading event was being carried out, the Indians would jump up from their hiding places and charge the soldiers. Men with the old-fashioned muzzleloaders did not have much chance against overwhelming numbers, but with breech loaders, Powell knew that a steady rate of fire from the quick loading weapons would slice the Indians to bits before they knew what had happened to them.

Powell also was prepared for a battle. He had trained his men for an event just like this, and with no element of surprise on their side the Indians would find a hornet's nest within the confines of the wagon box fortification.

That is just what happened. Red Cloud sent wave after wave of his finest warriors against the thirty-two men defending the wagon box corral. But, the sheet of flame and withering fire was too much for them. Even though the Indians were armed with rifles, they could not penetrate the wagon boxes and after fighting all morning and well into the afternoon, Red Cloud saw the writing on the wall and pulled his warriors back from the hot inferno. He had to, because Colonel Carrington pumped howitzer shells into the midst of his forces, scattering them with this small artillery fire as a relief force came to the aid of Powell and his men, who had defended their position so well.

While no one really knows, it is figured that nearly five hundred Indians were killed and wounded. Three soldiers were killed and several wounded. Against the massive odds against him, Captain Powell and his men fought one of the most courageous actions ever fought on the Plains. Powell was recommended for the Congressional Medal of Honor, but as far as it is known, he did not receive it. Red Cloud lost face with his people, although by the next year, after yet another treaty, he lived to see the hated forts along the Bozeman Trail abandoned.

THIS WAS THE DIFFERENCE ON AUGUST 2, 1867 - THE BREECH LOADING SPRINGFIELD RIFLE.
U.S.

Army Life in the West

It comes as no surprise when you ask youngsters of this generation how the soldiers looked and how they lived on western posts in the 1870s. Invariably, they will say that soldiers waved sabers, wore blue uniforms, lived inside of walled forts, and had Winchester repeating rifles, etc.

Of course, these kids are not to be blamed. But, Hollywood is to be questioned on how they have changed bits of history around to suit their fancy. Thus, errors are magnified by each succeeding Hollywood movie about the Indians and soldiers in the West.

Sabers, to set the record straight, were found to be a useless weapon on the plains of the West. Furthermore, they rattled and were a "danged" nuisance. Uniforms, at first were all polish and shine, but as the weather changed around and no big inspections were held in the field every day, it would not be too unusual to have seen a cavalry company riding across the hills outfitted in nearly everything but a bright blue jacket with brass buttons and highly shined boots.

The soldiers and their commanding officers adapted to the West in a hurry. One soldier said the only time he ever saw General Crook in a full dress uniform was the day they buried him.

Another item — few forts had log walls around them. The exception was Fort Phil Kearny near Story, Wyoming. Fur trading posts, long before the Army came west, had adobe and log walls, but few Army posts had them. In Wyoming between 1849 and 1890 there were some nineteen Army posts scattered around Wyoming, mostly along known trails like the Oregon Trail.

In 1870, a soldier's average pay was $13 per month. He worked hard in the spring, summer, and fall, when Indians found the grass to their liking and could carry out raids with plenty of feed for their horses. In the winter, Indians and soldiers stayed close to their fires.

In the winter of 1872, a soldier could look forward to a steady diet of beef. As a matter of fact, the menu at Fort Laramie was roast beef, gravy, and turnips for breakfast; bread, coffee, roast beef and gravy, mashed potatoes, and onions for lunch; and at supper he was fed stewed dried apples and pancakes with syrup and coffee. Not too bad; but I would guess it got to be tiresome. In fact, the post surgeon and post chaplain at Fort Laramie put out 6,000 strawberry, 250 raspberry, 250 blackberry, 100 currant, 600 asparagus, and 50 rhubarb plants in the post garden that year. Along with the change in diet, it helped prevent scurvy among the soldiers.

While there were not too many women out West at first, as soon as the Civil War was over, officers and ranking noncommissioned officers brought their wives and children to be with them on their tour of duty on the far-flung western posts.

While the Army was chiefly remembered for fighting Indians, it ought to be remembered that they had many other duties, too. They guarded emigrants and the trails they followed. They escorted stagecoaches, guarded railroad construction crews, protected the Pony Express and telegraph lines, and not to be discounted, their payrolls helped keep many a frontier community from going under when the building boom fell off. It was considered a real economic disaster when a post was closed down near a small town.

These men — most of them Americans, some from Ireland, Germany, Great Britain, and Canada — fought a ceaseless forty year battle with not only the Indians, but with the elements during their stay out West. And, even if they were not quite as glamorous as Hollywood would have us believe, they really were part of the drama and the romance of our stubborn struggle to inhabit what is now Wyoming.

The Rising Sun In the West

You might ask how the sun could rise in the West? Well, we are referring to the year 1876 when the Army of the Platte was commanded by General Phil Sheridan, who found among his many duties the handling of foreign military dignitaries taking a firsthand look at the Indian Wars on the Plains.

Thus, if you should have been riding on one of the stagecoaches running from Cheyenne to Deadwood in the fall of 1876, you would have seen the military pride of the country of the rising sun, Japan, taking in the rolling plains and mountains of old Wyoming as the guests of General Sheridan.

General M. Notu was the commanding general of the Japanese Imperial Army, and he brought General Fukushima and General

Tashoro along with their aide-de-camps to inspect the American Army in the West. They spent several weeks in Cheyenne, Fort Laramie, and Deadwood.

One tale about this imperial visit was told with tongue in cheek, I suspect, but it had to do with two Japanese captains running afoul of a trail crew of cowboys in Cheyenne.

Both Japanese officers, wearing their civilian clothes, were strolling along the streets of Cheyenne one evening when they were spied by a couple of Texas cowboys. Thinking the orientals were Chinese, the cowboys took down their lariats, shook out a loop, and caught up two indignant Japanese army officers. Hauling them back to where they had a couple thousand longhorns bedded down on the outskirts of Cheyenne, the cowboys proudly reported to their trail boss that their worries over locating a new trail cook were now solved. It seems their cook had just taken sick and had died.

Now, it was not uncommon for a trail crew or a cow ranch to have a "Chink" cook, as they called the Chinese cooks. Yet, I doubt if the trail boss knew that his new cooks were really Japanese officers, since neither officers could speak English, and certainly the trail crew knew nothing of Japanese. The mistake was pardonable, but General Sheridan was worried when he found the two missing.

But, Sheridan had to get to Deadwood to meet General Crook who was returning with this Big Horn and Yellowstone Expedition. So, he took the three Japanese generals with him, telling them that his men would find the missing officers, sooner or later.

At the same time, 2,000 head of longhorns were heading into the Black Hills where they were to be delivered to an Indian agent. The whole trail crew was bitter and near mutiny because their "Chinese" cooks could not fry a beefsteak, did not know the first thing about beans and bisquits, let alone how to boil an honest cup of coffee.

So, as they neared Deadwood, the trail boss paid off his two "Chinks" and hired a crippled miner who knew how to boil coffee and put on a pot of beans.

Thus, it was that the land of the rising sun provided cooks for the West and learned things about Wyoming no Japanese infantry drill manual had yet printed.

Both were so happy to rejoin their general officers that no charges were preferred, and when General Sheridan found out about the abduction, it is said he filed it away for future use, should he have to host foreign dignitaries who proved unwelcome.

The Grattan Massacre

It is hard to believe, but the theft of a single cow led to the slaughter of a young Army lieutenant named John Grattan and his entire command, amounting to twenty-nine soldiers and one interpreter, a few miles south of Fort Laramie on August 19, 1854. But it is true. A cow had been stolen from an emigrant caravan a few days earlier, and when the emigrants arrived at Fort Laramie, they reported the incident.

The post commandant, another lieutenant, ordered Grattan to take a detail of men in wagons down to a large Sioux encampment and either get the cow back, or bring in the Indian thief — preferably both. He was told to take a twelve-pound cannon with him and a small mountain howitzer as persuaders. And, since Grattan could not speak Sioux, an interpreter was assigned to him so he could convey his orders.

Only a few years earlier, thousands of Indians had agreed to let white men come into their country on their way West. Much big talk had flowed between the peace commissioners and the Indians. But no one, not even the white men, anticipated the overwhelming and seemingly neverending mass of humanity and wagon trains that plunged West.

Certainly, the Indians did not think they would have to deal with a situation like this — the cholera hurt them and killed them, a white man's disease. The emigrants killed off their buffalo, sold them bad whiskey, and shot at them in fright, even though they were trying to be friends.

On the other hand, young bands of wild Indians plundered unsuspecting wagon trains, kidnapped settlers, burned wagon trains, made off with cattle, horses, and oxen, and in general got so out of hand that the old chiefs who had made the Treaty of 1851 were almost powerless to call a halt to their savage depredations.

The Army got into the act in 1853 and had killed several Sioux, and whether it was a mistake as the Indians said, or right as the Army stated — the trouble had started. No one knew how to end it.

Put yourself in the place of young Lieutenant Grattan, a June graduate from West Point, and you must admit that his orders were nearly impossible to carry out. Nevertheless, down the river he went with his cannon, his howitzer, and twenty-nine men including a drunken interpreter who had boasted that the next time the Army came after the Sioux they would eat their hearts. That was the ultimate threat!

So, the Sioux, several thousand of them under Chief Bear and Chief Old Man Afraid of His Horses had a short pow-wow with Grattan. A fur trader named Jim Bordeau watched the proceedings from the top of his small cabin a half mile away and said later that the Army unit fired their cannon point blank into nearly one hundred Indians. The majority were along the river bank, or below the line of fire. Then they charged into Grattan, killing him and others with the rest of the soldiers fleeing back to the fort. Making short work of Grattan, the main body of Indians erupted over the river bank and pursued the rest of the soldiers, slaughtering them on the run.

With the taste of blood and killing, the young braves would not take heed of their leaders, and the rest of 1854 was a bad year along the trail. More soldiers under a field grade officer were sent to Fort Laramie, and in 1855 an expedition under the command of General Harney and Lieutenant Colonel Phillip St. George Cooke met a large Sioux band and fought them on Blue Water Creek in what is now Nebraska. Nearly one hundred Indians were killed with less than a half dozen soldiers being killed in the action.

However, the die was cast now, and for the next forty years, the Plains were ablaze with Indian battles and skirmishes. The Army could not let the Indians carry out these death dealing raids, and the Indians were fighting for their land. As it turned out, men of the Stone Age couldn't hope to win out over men of the Iron Age, even though Lieutenant Grattan and his men were early victims of the unavoidable war for the West.

The Big Horn Expedition

In the winter of 1869-1870 a meeting was held at the old McDaniels Theater in Cheyenne with the express purpose of forming an expedition to penetrate the Big Horn region in search of gold. The group who called themselves the Big Horners was headed up by Judge William Kuykendall. Colonel Farrar was second in command and Luke Murrin, a popular Cheyenne bar owner was made superintendent of the group.

Murrin's job was to organize, promote, and publicize the idea by going to Chicago and rounding up would-be gold miners and securing railroad fares for them into Cheyenne, where they would outfit the expedition. Murrin did go to Chicago, and he told some tales in that city that would stagger the imagination. Gold and silver, he allowed, were to be found in huge mother lodes all over the Big Horn Mountain area.

By the time he got back to Cheyenne in March, stories circulating around that city and in the local newspapers had it that several thousand men were ready, had the money to outfit themselves, and were just itching to see the spring snows melt away so they could shove off to discover gold and silver, and "git rich!"

While all this was going on, the commanding general of the Department of the Platte, which covered the territory the expedition had announced it was going to explore, worried that these men would damage earlier treaties made with Chief Washakie of the Shoshone Indians. General C.C. Augur shot off messages to Army posts in the area telling them to be ready for an invasion, since that is what the expedition looked like from all newpaper accounts.

Then, General Augur got a promise from Judge Kuykendall that the expedition would not get into the Wind River Reservation, which had been set aside for Washakie and his people. This agreement took off the edge of the expedition, because when it finally

HUGE
VARIETY OF
RIFLES
PISTOLS
GOLD IN
BIG HORN
EXPEDITION TO
SPECIAL RATES

left Cheyenne, instead of several thousand, there were only two hundred and seventy mounted men on the trail. Still, each was well armed and had a pack horse along to carry his extra supplies. It was a sizeable movement of men who finally arrived at South Pass City and the gold diggings there.

Gold had been discovered at South Pass in 1842, and while much gold had been taken from the mines, it was nothing like the Black Hills strike, which would occur a half dozen years in the future.

Rather than heading east to miss crossing the Wind River Reservation, the expedition went due north through the Indian treaty lands at the risk of breaking the treaty. Lucky enough, Washakie and his people were hunting in the Wind River Mountains at the time. But, after crossing the Owl Creek Mountains and dropping down into the area where Meeteetsee is now located, the expedition began to see smoke signals rising from the hills around them. They saw bits of mirror winking messages back and forth for the next few days. Their supplies were running low, and half of the men had not come with them from South Pass.

Besides there was no gold so far, even though they had panned every creek and stream they had crossed. Murrin's promises were bitterly cursed and a good many of the men, fresh from the civilized lights of Chicago, wished they had stayed at home.

But, the wily General Augur, knowing or guessing what these men might do, had sent a company of cavalry after them. So, when the soldiers caught up with the Big Horners, they were glad enough to turn around and get out of Indian country.

The *Daily Leader* in Cheyenne, one of the local newspapers, met the failure of the goldseekers with these words, "The key to the richest gold mines in Wyoming, or perhaps in the whole world, it seems is not yet within the grasp of white man." Little did the editor realize how prophetic his words were, because only a few short years were to pass before word came out of the Black Hills "Gold — from the grassroots down!"

Part Four
Cowboys & Cattlemen

Cattle and Their Brands

Let's face it, the cow has been mighty good to man. He, or I should say, she gives us milk and all the dairy products. We get leather and the multitude of products from leather. And we get beef, and boy how I like beef in just about anyway you can fry, bake, boil, broil, simmer, immerse, or treat it.

Sure, bones are used for other products, and I expect other saleable items come from the cow, too.

Even cowboys and their limitless escapades in books, poems, songs, stories, radio shows, television, art work, and motion pictures got their start from cows, too!

So, the cow developed the cowboy, and he had to have a particular type horse to ride after cows, so I guess you can say the cow developed the cow pony — quick on the turns, fast on the get-away, and tough as all get out.

In turn, the cow developed the rodeo, too. Because the rodeo got its start with cowboys who had learned to rope and ride after cattle. And, so the cow really got things moving out here in old Wyoming.

Remember, though, in order to claim your cows from other cowmen, you had to mark them, and that is where the branding came in with a particular brand of your own, registered with the state brand inspector now, or the cowmen's association.

Branding is not new. That got started in earnest with the Spanish and Portuguese back in the fifteenth century or thereabouts. And branding came to this country with their first cattle.

By the time cows started into what is now Wyoming, any cowboy could look at a herd of cattle and tell you who owned them and where they came from. He may not have had any real schooling, but he sure knew how to read brands.

Ear marking also is a part of branding. Why, you might ask, if they have already branded a cow? Well, simply put, the ear mark supplements the brand when the question of ownership arises because a brand can be altered to read, for instance from a circle dot brand to a wagon wheel brand. The ear mark will slow this down some.

That is stealing. Cattle stealing got pretty bad, but most of it was pretty well curtailed when the big stockmen's associations put out range detectives to keep a watch on the range. Between ear marks and brands, a rancher with the help of the association could put this worry behind him.

Right now, however, cattle rustling is still going on, and it is tougher today to stop than in past years. Modern trucks and trailers can stop, kill, and butcher a steer in mighty short order and sell the carcass out the back door in the next state right fast.

Consequently, Wyoming has more brand inspectors on the payroll than they did in the past, and these men, hard working former cowmen themselves, work long hours helping keep the brands, earmarks, and whose beef belongs to whom from those who are a shade on the other side of law and order.

What causes this? The price of beef, my friend. As I said in the beginning, nothing like a good beefsteak, and there are plenty of folks who will go to any end to get one laid out on their table.

How To Win An Election Without Really Trying

Very early in Casper's life, a most unusual mayor's election was held.

It seems a cowboy from down Wheatland way arrived in Casper with a herd of cattle. After selling and shipping them on the local railroad (the Fremont, Elkhorn and Missouri Valley Railroad) the cowboy dropped into one of the local saloons to wet his whistle.

While there he overheard a number of the locals talking about the election of mayor for Casper on the morrow. Innocently asking who was running, the popular local candidate was pointed out.

Well, one word led to another and as the evening waxed on, the cowboy and the candidate got into an argument, the grand finale of which was settled outside in the dusty, wide main street.

The cowboy won the scuffle, and was acclaimed an all-around fine fellow. As a matter of fact, several thought he ought to run for mayor. And, as he had never done this, he agreed to the act and by golly, when the returns came in the next day, Casper had elected a cowboy as their second mayor.

But, he had a cow outfit to run, and so he named a councilman as chairman of the council while he was away. It seemed a good idea, but as time wore on and months began to mount, it got to be a regular laughing matter that Casper had elected a mayor that not only did not live in Casper or Natrona County, but he had never attended one single council meeting.

What had seemed a popular and a good thing to do eight or nine months ago, now turned into a bottleneck nightmare for the city council. They could not act, and Casper was growing.

So, the council adopted a resolution to the effect that if any elected member of the council, and that included the mayor, was absent from three successive meetings without a reasonable excuse, the office he held would be automatically declared vacant.

As one Casper newspaper declared, "Casper enjoys the distinction of being a regularly incorporated and organized town, yet a town without a mayor. We've had no mayor during the past nine months; for, although a gentleman was elected to that position in the spring of 1890, he has ever since been a non-resident of the city. . . ."

Well, Casper managed to muddle along with the new resolution, and taking the jokes from all over the state, a city election was held in 1891 with Alexander Mitchell winning 69 to 64 over Peter C. Nicolaysen. Thus, a third mayor was installed in his office.

One note, both Mitchell and Nicolaysen owned land in Natrona county and the city, and they lived in Casper. The displaced cowboy mayor was elsewhere when the election was held. Some say he was shipping cattle in Colorado and did not learn he was not mayor of Casper for at least three months!

Old Time Rodeo

I know that people get tired of someone referring to the good, old days and a feller sayin' "Wal, back in those days we did so and so!" But in the case of modern rodeo versus the old time rodeo, I have got to say I would rather see an old-time rodeo than one of these modern over-commercialized affairs.

Frankly, I do not give a hang how many points one rider has over the other or what state in the Union he comes from. Neither do I care for steers, bulls, and horses that start moving when the chute gate opens and come to a dead halt when the timer's pistol shot is heard ending the time for the event.

What I would like to know is whatever became of the boot

race? Knowing most of the men entered, plus the pure fun of it could cause your sides to ache from laughing for a day or two.

Now, if you do not know what a boot race was, let me explain it. Cowpunchers lined their horses up behind a wire near where the judges held forth. They were dismounted and had already shed their boots into a large pile of boots about twenty yards away.

When the pistol sounded telling them to go, they headed for the pile of boots, trying to find their own, put them on, run back to their horse, climb aboard, and run around the track. First one home under the wire won. Sounds easy, doesn't it? Trouble came in heaps when a feller a leap ahead of you tried on a boot that was yours, found it did not fit, and then just plain threw it about twenty-five yards the other way. Didn't take thirty seconds before most boots were airborne and scattered in every direction, and tender footed cowpokes crowhopping all over the track trying to find his boots. Every once in a while, one of them cow waddies would lose his temper and punch a good friend right on the button, and sometimes it was really a better fist fight than boot race!

Another old-time race was the potato race. On board their trusty steeds, the cowpunchers were given sharpened sticks of equal lengths and at the word "Go" they raced half way down the track in front of the stands, stabbed their stick into a big boxfull of Irish spuds, and raced back to another box of their own where they shook off the potato. Then, they would turn around and do it again. The guy who had the most spuds inside his box at the end of the timed event, won a hatful of silver dollars.

Again, like as not, one of your friends would take his stick as you rode by with a spud firmly impaled on the end of it and he would take a swipe at your stick, knocking the potato off; and so, you would have to go back to get another. This was permissable, and even though fair in the judge's eyes, might cause some ruckus between the contestants. And it usually did. But it was fun, and the crowd and the contestants loved it.

Then, the egg race with a fresh egg shoved inside your mouth while you raced around the track; first one home with the egg still intact won the race. I knew a feller never won one of these races, but he always carried a bottle of beer with him so when he broke the egg, as he usually did, he could chase it with a cold beer.

Well, I do not expect the top rodeo hands today would want to ride for a hatful of dollars, but I would go on record that you, in the stands, would enjoy seeing some of the events from an old-time rodeo.

The Texas Trail

Tired and discouraged, the men from Texas who had fought for the Confederacy in the Civil War returned home to find times tough and money hard to locate. They did have one saleable item; nearly a million head of leggy longhorn cattle on the Texas range and an annual calf crop of nearly 750,000 — if they could find them! Their $5 cows would bring $50 each if they could get them to the Union Stockyards in faraway Chicago. The problem was how to get them there.

Anywhere from 800 to 1,000 miles north, railroads were bruising the hills of Kansas, Nebraska and Wyoming. If they could get their longhorns to a railroad, it would be no trouble to ship them to Chicago. So, they rounded up their herds and trailed them north to meet the railroads. It sounded simple. The only catch was taking a couple thousand head of mangy, stringy longhorns through Indian country, over dry land without water for miles and miles, fighting electrical storms, and hoping against hope that the herd you rode point on did not stampede.

One of the trails, named the Texas Trail for obvious reasons, came right into Wyoming past Cheyenne, Lusk, Gillette, and the Little Powder River region where it unraveled like a poor piece of rope as the herds moved east, west, and north at the end of the trail.

A typical outfit coming up the trail would look something like this: nine or ten hardened, lithe cowboys or trail waddies would drive a herd of about 2,000 longhorns, an old wagon with a cook and a span of long-eared mules carried grub and tarps for sleeping; the food consisted of tough beef, sorghum molasses, beans, flour, bacon, and coffee.

These cattle were the curly-haired Texans or Chinos; the Texan-Mexican breed that was calico colored with the long guant body; and a third type brought up the trail was also black and

white but not as wild as the longhorns themselves. The real longhorn was wild and had the long, slim blue horns. Not too heavy an animal, it was just "ornery" enough to survive a 900 mile trail drive and still bring a fair price at the railhead at Dodge City, Abilene, or Cheyenne.

Each man drew a different job. Heading up the crew was the trail boss with the cook playing an important role. The horse wrangler was in charge of the big herd of horses, and then usually about six or seven more cowboys. The fellow riding at the head of the herd was called the point, flankers rode beside the herd followed by swing riders and last, but certainly not least, the drag where a fellow ate dust from dawn until dark each day.

I doubt if the average person knows it now, but one of the meanest jobs was getting a trail herd to ford a river. If the sun was in the wrong position, that is low reflecting off the water, it blinded the cattle making it extremely difficult to get a herd to move. Johnny Lea, a leathery old trail boss, said he tried four straight days in 1883 to get a herd to cross the Yellowstone river. Another factor was that these cowpokes came from a land where water was scarce and few knew how to swim. It is surprising to note in the trail journals just how many cowboys lost their lives while trying to get a herd of longhorns to cross a river.

In the space of ten years herds coming up the trails out of Texas poured out nearly a million head of cattle into Wyoming and Montana. Fighting the elements, Indians, and a thousand other difficult situations, these men brought into Wyoming a new feeling so that today, the history and growth of our state is tied close to them. Yes sir, Wyoming is mighty proud of the fact that many of these cowboys settled down here and made their homes in Wyoming. That is why we call it the "Cowboy State" and proudly wear a bucking bronc on our automobile license plates.

Cowboy Capers

One of Charley Russell's most famous works of art shows a bunch of cowboys bunched up on buckin' broncs in front of an early-day saloon — trying to ride right into the log cabin bar.

That was a common occurence in those days and was looked upon as what the cowboy would try to do once he hit town.

It got so, a few years later, the town marshall frowned upon that sort of behavior. First off, the merchant or bar owner did not like it, and second, the West was growing up and there were other customers besides the high-heeled cowboy crew off a ranch.

But for a spell, the cowboy sort of called the tune when he hit town, because his was about the only payroll coming to town other than a handy military post, or a railroad crew going through.

When things sort of settled down and schools and churches came along with law and order, the cowboy still came to town, soaked up some redeye whiskey or tanglefoot — some called it popskill. Usually, he only made it to town three or four times a year and by that time he had hard cash in his jeans and a yearning for a good time — regardless.

After a day or two of riding up and down the main street, playing poker, dancing with the gals — he was winded, broke, and sick of town and was glad to go back to the open range.

Some of them died right in their hotel rooms when they just laid back on their beds and shot out the lights — gas lights, that is — from a prone position; and every now and then you read where a feller got throwed in the jug for shooting his steak with a sixgun 'cause it was too rare. . . .

After the big bath, then a shave and a haircut complete with Bay Rum, a new pair of Levi's, shirt, and all spic and span, the cowboy was up to just about anything.

In Cheyenne once, ten were jailed for trying to ride their horses into a roller skating rink. Then, there was always the argument in the bar as to which was either the best shot, the best fighter, or the best rider. Only one way to settle that argument — and that was to step outside and match up the claimants and let 'er go.

Broncs at best in a rodeo arena generally do not stop at a fence and a big window was no contest, or a boardwalk; and many a cowboy crew bent upon having their fun wound up facing a judge coughing up wages that came hard and were spent easy . . . for damaged furniture, broken windows, and the like. Trouble was, no cowboy was really a citizen of a community and sort of felt like he was not bound by all the city laws passed by a city council.

But — they always paid off. And one funny story is of a big guy sporting a heavy drooping mustache just coming off a big two-day spree in Lusk. He fell asleep in a local cafe while waiting for his last big meal before heading up to Hat Creek. While snoozing, his friends greased his mustache with limburger cheese. When the steak was set in front of him, he woke up and took a sniff of the meat. He declared it was bad and sent it back. Out came another steak. It, too, smelled bad. "In fact," the cowboy said, "the whole damn place smells bad." And he proceeded to let a little air into the cafe with his sixshooter; by then his friends were too scared to tell him the truth. And after paying the fine he got for shooting holes in the cafe, the tables, and his meal, he was let go. But, the judge said he had been "jobbed," and that if he wanted to get rid of the odor, he would also have to shave off his moustache. He did and, I am told, is still looking for the joker who coated his mustache with limburger cheese!

The Best Cow Country In the World

There is many an old-time cowhand who would gladly tell you that Wyoming, in its prime, was the best damned cow country in the world. 'Course that was before the fences got put up, law and order came, and people began to get civilized.

Did you ever wonder why Wyoming became so important to the history of cow outfits, growth of the cattle industry, and the eventual glamorizing of cowboys?

The prim professors in their classes will tell you that it was the almighty Union Pacific Railroad that reared the cow industry, but that is just not the whole truth. Sure, trailing a herd of cattle to market was surely helped by shoving them aboard the old boxcars and toting them back to Omaha or Chicago. And, it was not just to replace the buffalo that had been exterminated by bringing in Texas cows to feed reservation "Injuns."

It was just the plain nature of the country we know as Wyoming. Somehow, the grass was better. The Plains loaned themselves to great grazing areas. The mountains reared up and offered good summer range and a truly spectacular watershed. And — as one wit put it, "They weren't a fence 'tween Cheyenne and the Arctic Circle," which meant in driving blizzards cows could drift along with the wind and not pile up and perish at a fence line.

Then there were a series of stories and books written early about the fine range, easy land rights, great water, and mountains of money to be made out of raising cows in Wyoming. Those early-day promoters wrote their books and stories at just the right time, too.

You see, anthrax, a deadly disease struck down a major share of the beef herds in Europe and Great Britain. Since the British were a beef eating nation, they cast about for a new source of beef.

They read about it in a book written by a U.S. Army general named James S. Brisbin who had served in Wyoming in the 1860s.

His book entitled "The Beef Bonanza or How to Get Rich on the Plains" drew foreign investors to Wyoming like flies. They came in droves, and they were helped along with another writer by the name of Walter Baron von Richtofen, uncle of the famed Red Knight of Germany, a World War I flying ace. The Prussian lord, married to an English heiress lauded the West, Colorado, and Wyoming in particular, and soon the drawing rooms in Denver and Cheyenne were the scenes of English, French, Scotch, Irish, Welsh, and Prussian lords and ladies bent upon investing in cattle ranches out here. Easterners came from Boston and New York — and as one old cowboy put it — "We wuz loaded down with lords and lordlings."

Of course, the railroad helped, and so did the Indians needing beef on their reservations, and the invention of refrigerator cars helped — but in the end it was the never-ending grass, the sweet water, and the immensity of the land we know and love — Old Wyoming. Once those folks came, and many left within ten years, they left their stamp on Wyoming — the cattle business was off and running. Out of it grew the strong Wyoming Stock Growers Association, an organization that has played a very major role in the development of Wyoming, even today.

Now — nearly one hundred years later — we still have folks coming half way around the world to live in Wyoming — or from Boston and New York — to visit and live where the grass is still never-ending, the water still sweet, and the sky untroubled.

Cowboy Definitions

Every once in a while, I catch myself reading or hearing someone saying a word that I do not know, but pretend to know.

So, I thought maybe we would just sit here and clear up a few words I know you have heard, but do not really know what they mean.

Take barrel latch. Some of you will think that it refers to a rain barrel, or cider barrel. No. It is a gun barrel latch, and it held the barrel to the cylinder on a type of Smith and Wesson .44 caliber revolver used at Fort Apache in 1882.

How about a prairie belt? It sure as heck does not refer to a belt of agriculture. It was a type of heavy canvas belt used by soldiers out this way in 1870s with loops for heavy cartridges, caliber .50-.70. Three inches wide, these belts also had heavy bar buckels and a short leather tongue.

If you were a gunny, that is a good gun hand, you would have been an expert "can roller." You would delight in shooting at a tin can, and keep on hitting it and rolling it, never letting it stop. This was can rolling. A pretty fair shot in those days of the old West would take a brick and toss it into the air and break it in half. If you could do that in one shot, you would pass muster.

A coonie was a leather or cowhide stretched under a wagon bed, sometimes called a possum belly, into which a coosie, cowboy lingo for the Spanish word *cocinero*, or cook, would heave a good chunk of firewood every time he saw it as the chuck wagon rolled along a desolate and woodless prairie.

Oh, yes. A good gunny who could roll a can often fanned his gun. That does not mean, folks, that he waved a Chinese split bamboo fan over a hot barrel. It meant holding the six shooter in one hand and slapping the hammer back with the side of the palm or heel of the other hand.

Some cowboys preferred galluses, suspenders to you, to belts, and a large number liked to wear gaiters — a type of half boot to the calf high boot.

And while today we call them hippies, the really old-timers wore their hair shoulder length. Mountain men did at least, Army scouts and buffalo hunters could be counted on to have long hair, only touched once over lightly with the shears and not cut to the quick along the neck.

Lamps or lighting were usually found in two types, if you were talking about coal or oil or kerosene lamps. First off, there was the Argand type, with the wick all the way around producing a circle of light — the best light; or the second, with the flat wick. It would not produce half as much as the Argand.

Well, we did not cover much ground, but one of these days I will get around to some other funny things that were once commonplace and always held a prominent spot in the Old Monky Ward or Sears Roebuck catalog.

When Beef Was King

It was often said in Wyoming in 1880, when raising beef was a business you could not help but make money in, that if you started up a cow outfit one year, you lived on bacon, beans, and hard tack at first. The second year, you moved out of your dugout, built corrals and a log cabin, and hired two hands. The third year, you built a house, got married, and hired a foreman. The fourth year, you moved to Cheyenne, Lander, or Casper and let the foreman manage the outfit while the profits piled up in the bank.

Naturally, it was not that easy, but those years between 1870 and 1887 were the great years when cattle were in demand, the grass was free, and there were no fences between your outfit and the Arctic Circle. Fences were put up to keep chickens in the back of the ranch, not to separate your range from your neighbors, and Texas longhorns were pouring into Wyoming by the thousands each year.

The Union Pacific Railroad had finally gotten its tracks put down in good shape, and the year 1870 saw the first herd loaded out at Schulyer, Nebraska — sixty miles west of Omaha — headed for the fat beef market at Chicago. By 1880, cattle were being shipped from Pine Bluffs and Rock River, Wyoming, and their market was the French Army then involved in the tragic Franco-Prussian War.

In 1871, there were 70,000 cattle within a sixty mile radius of Cheyenne. Ten years later, there were nearly a half million scattered within the same radius.

What happened? What caused this big beef boom, this beef bonanza?

First, Texas cattle heading north to meet the railroads. Next, the demand for beef got caught up with the invention of the refrigerator cars and modern refrigeration methods. Couple these facts with the anthrax wiping out thousands and thousands of head of beef and sheep in Europe, and ready foreign capital was looking at the West.

But, above and beyond all these facts, probably one of the biggest growth factors was the winning of the Indian Wars. After Custer was wiped out, after Crook and Miles, and Reynolds and MacKenzie and others systematically pushed the Indians onto reservations, huge tracts of land in the vast area running from Casper north to the Canadian border opened up, and this was destined to be the beef range of the world for a number of years. In this vast territory the Sheridans, Buffalos, Miles Citys, and other cattle centers mushroomed into being and railroads moved in with the cattle.

The only thing that stopped the spiraling industry was the near fatal winter of 1886-87, a national panic, plummeting beef prices, and the farmers moving onto the public domain.

It was said of Teddy Roosevelt, who owned two ranches on the Little Missouri River — the Maltese Cross and the Elkhorn — stocked with $60,000 worth of cattle, that his foreman could not find a one in the spring of 1887. They were all dead.

The terrible snows had thawed, then froze over, and another big snow hit, and another thaw that froze and several more big storms hit. It was just too much. It broke the back of nearly all big and little cow companies, but not until beef had been king for nearly twenty years and had helped to bring Wyoming from a territory to a state during that period.

It was still a great country and an Englishman said, after reading of the great tracts open, "The immensity of the continent produces a kind of intoxication: there is moral dram drinking in the contemplation of the map. No Fourth of July orator can come up to the plain facts contained in the Land Commissioner's report." He was talking about Wyoming.

Black Frontiersmen and Cowboys

There has been a lot written about mountain men, explorers, soldiers, and cowboys, and just about always it is men from the South, the East, or West who have carried their share of glory.

Yet, I doubt if very many folks remember that a black man went with Fremont on his historic expedition of the West in 1843, and again with Fremont, in 1848. I also doubt if the average person realizes that over five thousand black men helped to bring cattle to the West from Texas, to build railroads, to string telegraph wire, and wore the uniform of the United States government in helping wrap up the Indian Wars in the West.

As one old-timer wrote, "We didn't care what the color of a man's skin wuz — we just wan't to be certain he could shoulder his share of the work with the cows." Thus, some of the very best cowboys were black, and their names deserve a niche alongside those immortal cowmen like Chisholm and others, because they too worked just as hard and died just as easily from the elements and a stray bullet or two as any white man or Mexican.

Besides York, who was with the Lewis and Clark Expedition, two famed mountain men were Jim Beckwourth who was at the Rendezvous in 1823 on the Green River in Wyoming with Ashley, and Ed Rose, who finally joined up with the Crow Indians and lived his life with them as a leader and chief.

I guess I enjoyed reading about Nat Love more than most, though, because he really lived quite a life on the range before trading in his cowpony for the iron horse and becoming a pullman porter. Nat grew up in Tennessee in the prewar years before the Civil War. When the great conflict was over, he got a job breaking colts, and soon earned a reputation as a real horseman.

By 1870, his reputation preceeded him and he wound up on the payroll of a Texas cow outfit headed for Kansas with 5,000 head of curly haired Chino longhorns. Before he got the job, the trail boss

told him he could go to work for him if he could ride the toughest horse in their cavvy of ponies. So, Nat climbed aboard a horse called Good Eye and plumb wore him out — and got the job.

From then on, his life was just one big heap of escapades after another, first with the Indians, then with gunfighters, and then as an early-day rodeo star. In fact, he was the man who won the title as all around cowboy at the very first Deadwood Days in the Black Hills and claimed the title as Deadwood Dick until the day he died. There were, of course, many men who claimed they were Deadwood Dick, the gunman and bank robber. Nat claimed his title on board the tossing deck of a wild-eyed bronc the Fourth of July, 1876 — just a few weeks after Custer met his defeat a couple of hundred miles west of the Black HIlls.

Nat remembered that this contest was between six cowboys who had to rope, tie, throw, saddle, and ride a mustang. He completed his task in just under nine minutes and gathered a prize of $200 for his efforts. Then, they shot for skill, and Nat took this prize, too. Thus, the title Deadwood Dick, a man every person — black or white — could be proud of who helped build the West.

"Come An' Git It!"

I guess about the most welcome sound a cowboy ever heard was "Come an' Git It!" It meant only one thing — food, grub, chow — and it could be a crispy dawn breakfast of hotcakes and coffee so strong and black it could float a .44 caliber bullet. Or, it could be beans, bisquits, and beef.

Usually, it was bread — that is, sourdough and a slab of beef you might have to wrassle around a bit before you got it all down — but it was hot, and it was good, and it was nearly always on time.

The range cook was the chef of the prairie and the mountain. He could build a meal out of nearly anything and usually did just that. He most always had anywhere from five to ten men to feed, depending upon the size of the outfit he worked for.

His word was law around the chuck wagon and the dutch ovens and frying pans. He could call down the wrath of the Good Lord on an erring cowpoke; one who got to chow late, or rode a pony near his feed box, or forgot to haul in wood for cooking.

So, everyone, from the owner of the outfit down to the lowest paid jingle bob on the payroll, walked softly around the range cook.

Couple of years ago, I had a visit with a friend over in the Big Piney area as he was moving five-six hundred head of cows. I drove up, walked out, and met him in the middle of a sagebrush covered flat. While we were talking, his oldest son drove up in a pickup, fished out a couple of cold, greasy hamburgers and two beers — and that was lunch. We laughed about it. He told me that they just could not find cooks anymore.

And that's right. As I drove off, I remembered one old cook who used to set up a regular meal that cooked while he was gone. He would take some canned tomatoes, cut up some roast beef, throw in some beans and anything else loose around camp. Put all this in a cast iron pot and put the lid on while he jammed the whole affair into hot coals. When it got to bubbling real good, he would take a stick, lift the pot, and place it into an ammunition box lined with clay and straw and then leave it. It would continue to bubble and simmer for a long, long time. Then, when he came back from wherever he had gone, his "wife" as he called it, would have completed cooking the meal and with little or no preparation, he could sit down to just about one of the best stews you ever laid your lips around.

I know, because I have eaten that type of stew a time or two myself.

Once when I was just a little kid up where Meadowlark Lake is now in the Big Horns, a roundup crew was gathered around a chuck wagon waiting for dinner. The old cook watched me while he carved up man-sized chunks of beef, slapped them down on a flat piece of iron stretched out over a huge pile of red hot coals, and seared steaks. Then he would fry a couple on huge frying pans, and run in some flour and water to make pan gravy, or "sop," as he called it.

I tell you the smell would create an appetite in a dying man. Anyway, he finally said, "Yunker, we always invite people to eat at our outfit. So, grab a plate and name yore steak. I onlys want you to scrape your plate clean and then help me wash up afterwards."

I never ate a steak before or since that tasted better! And, I probably never washed more tin plates and coffee cups. But, it was worth it, and I only wish my own kids could suffer the same sort of treatment in their life, but I am afraid those days are long gone.

Part Five
Both Sides of the Law

String 'em Up

It got so bad during the last twenty-five years of the nineteenth century in Wyoming, that vigilante committees were formed and the familiar words "String 'Em Up" resounded from every section of Wyoming.

Gold camps and the lure of nuggets as big as walnuts, leather pokes stuffed with fine gold, and strongboxes, with weak locks, brimful of gold were the magnets that drew every size and shape of badman to Wyoming.

Not only gold, but the slow moving railroads were easy targets for the mounted badmen who, once they held up a train, could move in almost any direction and get clean away from the posses, who generally got on the trail anywhere from one to five days later.

Besides, Jessie James and his gang had given all railroads a bad name, and it was popular to hold up a railroad. Same with banks, and Army payrolls. All three were easy targets for mounted hold-up artists.

Probably the toughest work for a badman was cattle rustling. First, there was just no easy place to ship the beef, and townsmen were the best organized units in the West. Second, the cowboys were nearly all armed and tough, or even tougher than the bad guys. And finally, beef did not bring the fast return that a poke full of gold did in a small western town, where few questions were asked as long as you could keep on paying the bill.

Law and order had its hands full, and some of the citizens got tired of waiting around for justice to take care of their problems.

The hanging of Cattle Kate and her boy friend, Jim Averell, was a classic example of local justice.

Another example was the hanging of Jack Slade up in Virginia City, Montana Territory. Good enough guy when he was sober, Slade was every inch a tough hombre when drunk. And, he drank a lot.

When he hit town, he terrorized the community of Virginia City. No one was safe and after his spree, he always made amends in payments to the store owners whose windows he had shot out, the bars he had wrecked, and so on. But, there were those who finally got tired of Slade and his rowdy friends and one day, captured the badman, strung him up — and that was the end of Slade.

Simple, but unlawful justice. It served its purpose though, and the rest of the toughs left town.

Down in Rawlins they did the same with Big Nose George Parrott. He had killed a couple of popular young men from Carbon, made good his escape and wound up in Montana. The sheriff from Rawlins heard about where Big Nose was, and went up and captured him alive.

When he brought him back to Rawlins, a vigilante group stopped the train and threw a lariat over a telegraph pole and tried to hang George. But when they kicked the box from under him, his feet hit the ground. So, they gave up and the sheriff put him in jail. A few weeks went by, and again the vigilantes broke into the jail and tried to hang the badman. Not being professionals at it, they again miscalculated and George really did not get hanged. Back in jail, a thoroughly broken badman now, Big Nose George was again taken by a mob who by now had hanging experience and they got the job done — finally!

The arrival of strong sheriffs and marshalls like Malcolm Campbell, Frank Canton, and Joe LeFors got law and order back on even keel by the turn of the century.

Tom Horn — Good or Bad?

Over seventy years ago, on November 20, 1903, Tom Horn was hanged in Cheyenne. His crime? Killing a fourteen year old boy named Willie Nickell who was wearing his father's hat and slicker, and riding his father's saddle horse.

It is said that Horn had been hired to get rid of the father, a bothersome rancher who had been in a knife fight with John Coble, owner of the big Iron Mountain Ranch.

Whatever the case, it is true Nickell cut Coble pretty badly with a stock knife, and later on, following the shooting death of his son, Kels Nickell was shot at a number of times as he rode unarmed and zig-zagging through an alfalfa field to his home. He was hit in the left arm, shattering the bone near the elbow; once in the hip; and the third shot nicked him under the right arm.

While the first case, the killing of the boy, was finally laid at the feet of Horn, the second shooting was blamed upon Jim Miller and his sons August and Victor. But, they were let go when they proved they could not have done the shooting.

The Nickell killing and the Nickell shooting were to remain a mystery for quite a spell. The year was 1901, and while no one proved Tom Horn was involved, his reputation and the killings he was credited with, surely gave him the credit.

Away up in the Big Horn Basin, kids who defied their mothers by not coming when she called them for supper as the evening sun dropped behind the hills would be told, "One of these days Tom Horn will get you, if you don't come in before dark." And, I am told on good authority, in this case my own father who was ten years old at the time, that the threat was more than enough of an inducement to scare the pants off the average Wyoming kid.

Horn, who had piled up an honorable record as a Pinkerton agent in the Colorado-Utah region, kept it going with good work for stockmen in Wyoming. He was an outstanding packer in the Spanish-American War. But it was his record of killings after the war that caused fear to strike at the heart of any rustler once he had reason to believe Horn was on to his trail.

Liked by his close associates, Horn was a legend in his own time. It was said that once he had killed a man, he lifted the head and placed a small rock under it, thus giving notice that this was a Horn execution. Few people killed by Horn were innocent of the crime of cattle rustling, or other crimes.

My guess is that Horn was a professional killer. He always used a rifle at long range, and he rarely missed his man. And, he killed for money.

When they hanged him, where Cheyenne Federal Savings and Loan Office is located today in downtown Cheyenne, he was the coolest hand there and that means among the spectators, the reporters, the military, the law officers, and the prisoners looking on.

Yes, Tom Horn was a cool hand. But, like most cool hands bucking the laws that govern society, they wind up dangling from a gallows, or are served some other form of justice for their lawlessness.

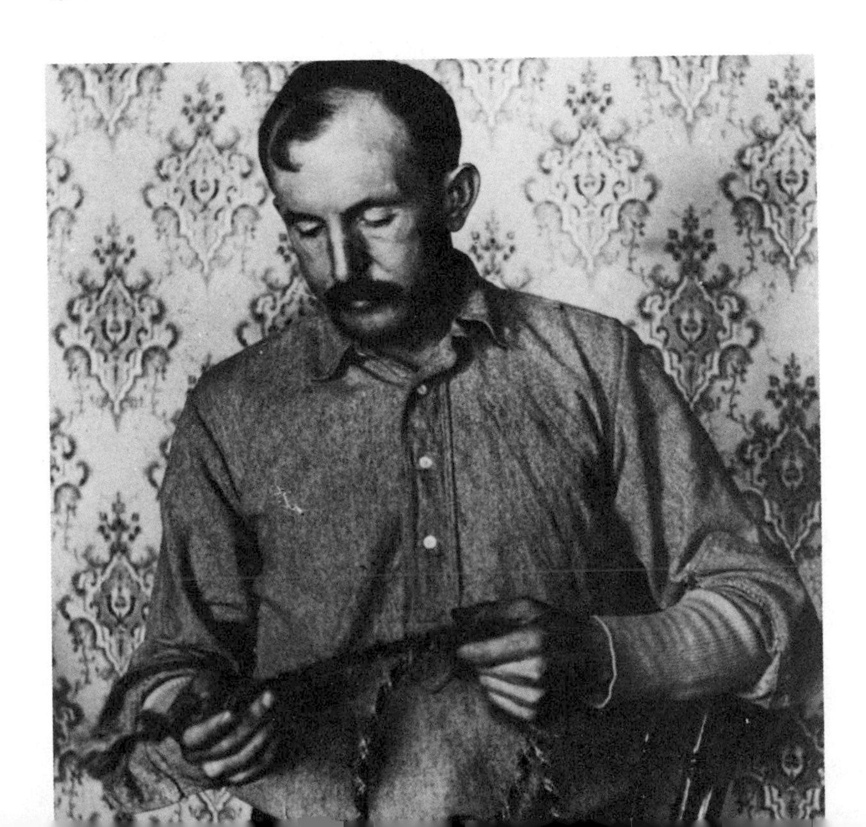

Bob Dalton in Wyoming?

When I was about twelve years old, my Dad introduced me to Emmett Dalton out in Los Angeles. He was the last of the famous Dalton Gang. He collected twenty-three bullet holes in his hide at Coffeyville while trying to hold up a bank. That was in 1892. I met him in 1936, the year before he died.

He came from a family of fifteen children, and before it was all over — most of the boys had died following a life of crime. Emmett survived, wound up in California, wrote a book, and naturally, was hired by Hollywood as a technical director on a number of western motion pictures dealing with bank holdups.

Now, I do not know if any of the Daltons ever rode in Wyoming, but I ran across a story about Bob Dalton holing up in the Buffalo country in the late 1880s. Here is the story — fact or fiction — I like it.

Seems as if three men rode up to this small ranch being run by a semiretired doctor by the name of Edward W. Huson. They were covered with dust, tired, and one of them was plumb busted up. Someone had evidentally told them Huson was a doctor, and it was to him they brought their wounded partner. Then, they rode off and left him.

All this took shape about the time one of the Deadwood stages carrying a load of gold dust to Cheyenne had been held up.

Time went by, and the man laid up began to mend. His manners were the very spirit of Southern gallantry. No one in the Huson house had cause for alarm — especially, the sons of Dr. Huson. They literally worshipped the stranger, would run errands for him, and avidly listened to his stories of the range and plains.

Then, as all things do, it came time for the stranger to ride on. He settled up with his benefactor and wife by peeling off a couple of

$100 bills from his money belt for their hospitality and medical work.

Then he called the young sons of Huson over and told them that he was Bob Dalton. Said he was just a no-good train robber and outlaw. And, he advised them never to get their money the dishonest way.

He said he had something real bad happen to him, and all the while he was laid up, the bad thing kept coming back to him.

He said he had held up a stage his mother was riding on. She had come out to see him, and he, unknowingly held up that very stage. Said he had not seen her in ten years, had no way of knowing she was on that very stage that he had held up, and nearly scared her to death.

She was terribly upset, but he did not have the courage to tell her he was the holdup man. He said she tried to get him to come home to Kansas and get away from this wicked country. He gave her some money and sent her home.

"But, men, I lied to her," he said and he told them it was a real bad thing — having to lie to his mother.

Then, he rode off.

Now, I do not know if it is true — but one thing I do know. Bob Dalton died at Coffeyville with his brother Gratt while Emmett took the twenty-three holes in his hide. But, I never heard of a Huson going bad. So, I guess the story bears repeatin'.

Sheriff Campbell

Malcolm Campbell was my kind of sheriff. So was Frank Canton and Al Sproul. Nothing fancy about them, let the boys have their fun and when the going got to getting a little too tough, they stepped in and cooled the young hotheads off, brought sense back to the older ones, and generally ran a pretty good town and country.

Malcolm Campbell was sheriff in Douglas during its heydays, when Fort Fetterman was more than a name on a tourist's lips, when Tent Town was the biggest town in Converse County, and when the effects of the Johnson County War were sweeping across Wyoming hills and valleys.

He had been born and raised in Canada, came to Nebraska and worked on the Union Pacific, freighted up and down the whole Cheyenne-Laramie-Rawlins-Fort Laramie and Fetterman area, before he settled down and became a deputy sheriff.

No question about whose side he choose in the Johnson County War. He felt the cow companies were getting no justice and that they were being stolen blind. He made no bones about his dislike for "Red" Angus, sheriff up in Buffalo, and while the war was rocking along, Campbell found plenty to do in Douglas and did not spend too much time stopping folks wearing side arms on their way north.

But he was a fair man, a product of the frontier, and one you could count on.

Frank Canton had got whipsawed in the early fighting in the war that was to take place in Johnson County and had wound up leaving Buffalo and coming back with the invaders.

He eventually got caught with the invaders and spent the best part of the spring and summer of 1892 traveling from Cheyenne to Laramie and back to Cheyenne along with forty-five other men waiting for a trial that never came off.

Still in all, he was a good man, and if Malcolm Campbell said he was alright, then you could tighten your cinch on that for life.

Al Sproul replaced the infamous Angus as the new sheriff of Johnson County and had quite a job in cleaning out the rustlers living in that part of Wyoming.

While I know for certain he never heard of John Wayne, the cowboy movie actor, I bet Wayne has heard of Sproul, because he acted out a scene in a movie that could only have come from Sproul's life.

Seems like Sproul had to serve warrants on two real hard cases for stealing cattle. One was the father and the other was the son. Both were named, and Sproul drove to the ranch, left his deputy in his wagon, walked into the ranch house and started reading the warrants. The father drew his sixgun while Sproul was reading and so did the son, from behind Sproul.

When the shooting stopped a fraction of a second later, both outlaws were dead and Sproul holstered his shooting irons and carried the bodies out, slung them into the wagon and drove off unconcerned, or so his deputy said later on! Sproul was a real he-man and helped make his county and Wyoming a better place to live.

The Hole In the Wall Gang

As far as the average citizen of Wyoming went in 1897, he had not heard too much about Butch Cassidy and the Sundance Kid. What he was worried about was what Bob Divine, foreman of the CY cattle outfit, was going to do up in the Hole In The Wall country when he invaded that piece of Wyoming real estate.

No, sir. Few people even knew Cassidy or the Kid, notwithstanding the movie of recent years.

The Hole was a break in the wall of red sandstone that separated the Big Horn Mountains from the plains and Powder River breaks. Buffalo Creek runs along this wall until it finds a natural outlet through the wall, thus the title, Hole In The Wall.

Bob Divine led a dozen cowboys into that region where he figured cattle from his and other cow outfits were being taken, rebranded, and then sold north over the Montana border.

A small range war was fought near the Hole In The Wall Ranch, just south of the famed Bar C Ranch. It turned out Devine and his men had a real shoot-out with three men — Bob and Al Smith and Bob Taylor.

In the action, it was reported that more than a hundred rounds were fired between the opposing cowboys, and that Bob Smith was killed. Devine's horse was killed, Devine himself was slightly wounded and his son, Lee was wounded. Al Smith had his handgun shot out of his hand and his thumb nearly shot off and several others were nicked by angry lead.

While many will think these men were bad shots, you have to remember the battle was fought on board the heaving deck of a horse. The fight lasted only a few minutes during which time horses were pitching, bucking, and rearing as each rider thumbed back his six shooter and threw hot lead at moving targets.

When Bob Smith stopped the killing bullet, the battle ended. Both sides retired. For all intents and purposes the fight was over.

At first, Devine — who actually killed Smith — was going to be tried in a Natrona County court, but it was changed to Johnson County, since the killing occurred in that county. Devine gave himself up, was placed under bond, but officers of both counties let the matter drop figuring that it was a fair fight, and a cooling off period might stop what could turn into a real range war.

A month later, Devine rounded up twenty-seven cowboys in August and again invaded the Hole In The Wall after cattle he figured rightly belonged to the CY outfit. Men from the Ogallala cow ranch east of Casper, Pugsley's ranch in Converse County, and several independent cowboys went with Devine.

While they were observed and did gather about two hundred head of stray cattle, their number was so large that no fight took place.

Later on Butch Cassidy and the Sundance Kid did use the Hole In The Wall country to hide out, but not until the turn of the century.

Whatever Happened To Joe LeFors?

Whatever happened to Joe LeFors? Well, first off about half of you reading this will ask, who was Joe LeFors? And, the other half will wonder what did happen to this fine man?

Joe LeFors was one of Wyoming's better known lawmen. He is the guy who finally got the evidence on Tom Horn, the hired gun for some large stockmen in the southern end of the state, and this evidence led to the hanging of Horn in Cheyenne on November 20, 1903, for the killing of a young boy named Willie Nickell.

The answer to the second part is that Joe LeFors passed quietly away in his home in Buffalo on October 1, 1940.

But, there was more than just the Tom Horn case in LeFors life. He had been a Pony Express rider, he had been a stock detective, he had cowboyed with the best of them, wound up a brand inspector, and finally was a model U.S. Marshall. Some folks even say that the "Whispering Smith," often used in motion pictures, was modeled after Joe LeFors. It could be the truth.

Let me tell you two stories about LeFors that will tell you what kind of man he was.

With lots of rustling taking place in the Newcastle area, he pulled up in a draw one day in 1896 and watched while a man unloaded a rifle from his wagon, and then shot and killed a yearling. LeFors said later, "It was a nice shot."

Then, as the man skinned out the critter, he approached and arrested him, saying that since the hands of the culprit were covered with blood, he had really caught him "redhanded!"

He let him go back to his small, tumble-down cabin to change clothes before taking him in for arrest. Seeing his wife and small kids in a sad condition, LeFors asked how they were doing. She showed him about five pounds of flour and nothing else — no bank book — no food. LeFors just climbed aboard his horse and rode off. Two days later, he came back and the family had left, but without a record following them and when LeFors told the owner of the killed yearling, he was plumb satisfied.

Another story tells how he caught a real cattle thief. He got a confession from him; took him to the L Open AK owner, whose cattle had been rustled, and the thief confessed. The owner cooked a breakfast for the thief, whose brother had joined them, and before it was all over, the cattle had been returned and the two men had settled down to a long and steady job.

Yes, LeFors was a lawman and with that kind of justice and the reasonable thinking behind him, he saved the county and the state lots of money for jailing people as well as many a heartbreak. You might also say, he straightened out some men who might have really turned bad.

He was a credit to his profession — Joe LeFors.

The Cowboy Detective

It got so bad in the 1880s that it was hard to tell the good guys from the bad guys. I am speaking about cattle rustling, horse stealing, and gunslinging.

And Wyoming was sure no bright spot during that period. It seemed as if every cowboy drifter out of a job or running ahead of the law for a crime committed elsewhere, wound up working for one of the big cow outfits somewhere in Wyoming.

Many of the really big cow companies were owned by rich eastern or foreign interests who cared little for the personal side and pride of a good outfit. Thus, a good many of these "wanted" men signed on for a period of time, or until they felt the law had forgotten their crime.

One old-time cowman told me that times were pretty tough for a plain cowboy, and many was the time that wages just were not paid at all from November through April. Oh, you could stay on, work around the main ranch, eat good food, and sleep in a warm bunkhouse — but no pay except there was always the promise of wages in the spring. This, my good friend told me, was one of the reasons why so many cowboys started stealing cattle, branding big calves, or rebranding and cutting ears so they could start up herds of their own. When a man was found out, and even though he could not be jailed for it, he was blackballed and fired. Being blackballed meant no member of the Stock Growers Association would or could hire you.

This cattle rustling continued on through the 1880s until it finally erupted in the Johnson County War. The big cattle outfits had to do something about the rustling or go out of business. The little cowman had his side of the story, too.

But one fellow seldom heard about was the range, or cowboy detective. Usually you hear about a sheriff, a marshall — a Joe

LeFors — but due to the nature of his work, not too much was ever written about the cowboy detective.

One fellow worked at this profession for nearly thirty years before retiring in New Mexico. He was hired by a regular agency who trained him in his work, that is, how to write reports, give evidence, what evidence would stand up in court, and so forth. Of course, he had to be a real cowboy, know all the ropes so to speak, or his detective work, which was normally undercover, was quickly spotted by suspicious outlaws.

One time, he was assigned the job of bringing to justice five or six known Texas outlaws wanted for murder, bank holdups, and cattle rustling, who were hiding out on a Wyoming ranch. The year was 1887 when the detective rode up to the ranch where they were "holed" up. He came in walking, or limping, claiming his horse had thrown him. He had recently been shot through his right knee, thus had a built-in limp made to order. With his six shooter strapped in a shoulder holster under his heavy shirt, and a throwing knife stashed in his left boot top, the detective was looked upon with suspicion at first. As his "limp" healed itself, and the outlaws found he was a pretty fair shot, could speak their language, he was soon welcomed into their midst. But, it took a long six months of hard riding, hard living, and quick thinking before the detective was able to get enough evidence on the men so that a sheriff's posse surrounded the ranch and jailed the whole crew. Out of eleven men arrested, ten of them were given long jail terms. Only one got off because the prosecuting attorney could not prove anything on him.

Guess who that was? You're right. The cowboy detective, who went on to help rid the range in Wyoming and elsewhere from criminals and outlaws.

"Hands Up!"

One passenger riding the stagecoach from Deadwood to Cheyenne in 1877 arrived sporting a watch chain made up entirely of gold nuggets over two feet long. The nuggets ranged in size from a pea to a good average walnut. The next week, one of the treasure coaches arrived with over $25,000 in gold dust in its strongbox.

Small wonder that the Black Hills stage was held up day after day through 1876, 1877, and 1878 with a sort of clocklike precision. Gold strikes always drew unsavory characters — crooked gamblers, painted ladies, and the like — and along with them, a number of holdup artists whose "Hands Up!" got to be a familiar phrase.

But, the gold discovery in the Black Hills drew more than the usual number of road agents, bandits, outlaws, and holdup men.

First, there was an almost unlimited supply of gold pouring down out of the hills to Cheyenne — lots more than the usual strike. Next, it was tough to get the gold dust out of the hills in the winter, so it was saved up and brought out in what was termed as a spring cleanup. That meant large supplies of gold were brought out all at once. Then too, the trip to Cheyenne was nearly three hundred miles long, and drifting down through the rolling hills between Deadwood and Cheyenne were literally hundreds of places that were ideal in terms of holding up a stage.

The stage line devised all sorts of ways to stop these masked and sometimes, unmasked bandits. They designed a "salamander," an absolutely steal proof strongbox. But, it was broken into. They even built a coach which was nearly all steel and iron and called it the "Monitor." But, that coach was held up, too. They had soldiers ride alongside as escorts, sometimes they even rode inside the coaches. They used shotgun guards, outriders, men riding ahead, men riding behind the coaches; but still the holdups went right on occurring.

It got so bad in 1878 that one coach was held up three different times on one run by three completely different gangs. Money, jewelry, and personal items were taken the first time. Guns, and mail the second time. And the third time, the bandits took clothing and baggage so that the occupants of the coach arrived at the stage station in their winter underwear.

Three things served notice on gangs led by Stuttering Smith, Dunc Blackburn, and Big Nose George. First, a holdup artist got into the mail, and this was a federal offense. So, special agents from the government arrived on the scene. Next, men like Johnny Slaughter, Quick Shot Davis, and others were riding as shotgun guards. They were fearless, well paid, and would not hesitate to shoot first and ask questions later. Holding up a coach got to be right dangerous. And, finally, vigilante gangs began to spring up and take action into their own hands.

One such action occurred when "Dutch" Charley was taken from Rock River to Laramie. En route a band of masked men took him from the law officer and hanged him. It also happened over at Rawlins where vigilantes removed Big Nose George Parrot from the local jail and strung him up.

The heat was too much, and little by little the gangs drifted away where law and order, vigilantes, and federal agents were not riding side-by-side so that a holdup man could not be sure just who he was trying to steal from.

Butch Cassidy's Legal Beagle

When Butch Cassidy, alias George LeRoy Parker, was apprehended and jailed for horse stealing in the Lander area in 1894, he sent for Douglas A. Preston, Wyoming's leading and most prestigous criminal attorney to defend him against the charges.

It was an open and shut case. The leader of the Wild Bunch was destined for Wyoming's big house at Laramie, but Preston gave him a real ride for his money, and Cassidy never forgot it.

Thus, when his old buddy Matt Warner got a little drunk, went on a toot in Utah, and got into a gun spree during which he wasted one guy, blew the leg off another, and punched air holes with his Colts .44 in a third, he sorely needed a good attorney.

He told Cassidy, "I need help. Over here in Utah, they 'twitch 'em!" He was referring to gallows lingo for a hanging. In Wyoming, a legal hanging was done at a gallows with a trap door. Most condemned would rather take the straight and unexpected drop as a life exit. In Utah, they stood them on top of a big, box-like structure, then kicked it out from under the man standing on top with a rope around his neck. When he hit the end of the rope, he "twitched," or danced the dance of death.

So, Warner wanted legal help to keep from twitching, and Cassidy got ahold of his legal brains, Preston. No trouble to help Warner, but he would have to get help from two top criminal attorneys in Utah, and that took lots of money.

Some say that is what precipitated the daring daylight robbery that Cassidy, Elza Lay, and Bob Meeks pulled in the spring of 1896 at Montpelier, Idaho. They took $16,000 and in evading the posse, Cassidy found the oates bags full of silver dollars too heavy and hid several of them somewhere in Star Valley where they remain today. The rest he used to hire Preston and his Utah team, and to help Warner's wife and small daughter, Rose.

Preston got Warner a five-year sentence, and his fears of "twitching" in Utah were stilled.

Looking back on the Lander sentencing, one finds Cassidy standing before the bar of justice with the presiding district judge being Jesse Knight, one of the men who signed the Wyoming Constitution and who went on to become chief justice of the Wyoming Supreme Court.

Melville C. Brown of Laramie helped Preston, and he had been the president of the Wyoming Constitutional Convention, and he too went on to become chief justice of the Wyoming Supreme Court.

The prosecuting attorney was just starting out, and he had Judge Samuel T. Corn helping him out as there were so many criminal cases on the docket. Judge Corn was also a long-time member of the Wyoming Supreme Court.

The prosecutor was young William L. Simpson, the father of Milward L. Simpson, a Wyoming attorney who served as a governor and a U.S. Senator of Wyoming. His son, Alan Simpson, is now a U.S. Senator from Wyoming.

And Preston? Well, he held posts in both the State House of Representatives and the Wyoming Senate in later years. He ran in 1914 against Congressman Frank Mondell for Congress, but got beat. He was to be the Wyoming Attorney General under Governor Robert Carey, and under Governor John B. Kendrick from 1911 through 1919. Oh, yes, Preston also was one of those men who signed the Wyoming State Constitution. And he was Butch Cassidy's legal beagle!

Wyatt Earp In Wyoming

The first time Wyatt Berry Stapp Earp saw Wyoming he was with his father and mother and five brothers and two sisters. The year was 1864, and his father had resolved to move from Illinois to California. A veteran of the Mexican War, and the Civil War, old Nicholas Wyatt was looking for new frontiers. He had been wounded in the war between the states, and he felt California would be a good place to start over again.

He had named his fourth son after his commanding officer, Colonel Wyatt Stapp Berry. On the trip to California he realized that Wyatt was a top man when it came to handling horses and mules. Years later, Wyatt Earp was to say that between Fort Laramie and Fort Bridger, he helped fight off a half dozen raids on the wagon train by Indians. It was the first time he ever pointed a rifle or pistol at another human being, and shot at them with the intent to kill.

He was to follow that trade as a paid gunfighter-frontier marshall for the best part of his life.

Four years later, he came back to Wyoming as a twenty year old contractor with a number of mule teams plowing up sod ahead of the fast tracklaying squads of men building the Union Pacific Railroad. On the Fourth of July, 1868, Wyatt Earp turned up in Cheyenne holding the wagers of a couple of hundred men who had sent him to bet their money on Wyatt's choice between a prize fight staged between Mike Donovan, a classy heavyweight, and young Johnny Shannessy, a newcomer to the ring. Earp had fought his way into prominence at a number of brawls in the tent towns along the railroad right of way and was looked upon by the hard-fisted Irish tracklayers as a good man, honest and a firstrate judge of fighting men.

Earp looked the fighters over, and cast his lot with Donovan. It is a matter of record that Shannessy took the beating of his life, and that Earp returned to Bear River City, Wyoming Territory, with his money belt bulging with well bet money for his friends.

Eight years later, he took off the winter of 1876-77 from his rugged duties as town marshall of cowtown Wichita, Kansas, and took his brother Morgan with him to see if they could prospect and find gold in the Black Hills. He did not make any money in the gold mines, but he and Morg gathered together a couple of teams of horses, and hauled wood for fuel to an ice-cold Deadwood that had forgotten to lay away a supply for winter.

That spring, when the big shipment of gold bullion was being shipped out of Deadwood to Cheyenne, Luke Vorhees and "Quick Shot" Davis hired Morg and Wyatt to ride shotgun on the treasure coach of the Cheyenne and Black Hills stage line.

Road agents cached themselves outside of Deadwood and methodically held up incoming coaches carrying mine payrolls, and took their share of gold dust coming out of the hills. So, the Cheyenne and Black Hills Stage Line took an ad in the Deadwood and Cheyenne newspapers announcing that Earp was riding guard:

NOTICE TO BULLION SHIPPERS

> The Spring Clean-Up will leave for Cheyenne on the Regular Stage at 7:00 A.M. next Monday. Wyatt Earp of Dodge, will ride shotgun.

Besides getting their trip to Cheyenne free, both Morg and Wyatt earned $100 each for the trip. Naturally, the gold arrived in Cheyenne in good shape.

And, while he and Morg were in Cheyenne, Wyatt was a witness to a classic street gunfight that took place at sixteenth and Logan, or just in front of the Dyer House Hotel.

The argument arose over a gambling debt between Charlie Harrison and Jim Levy. Wyatt knew both men, and he used the results of the fight over the years as an example of how to win and save your life, or lose and be dead.

He told men betting on the outcome of the fight not to put their money on Harrison, who was the quick draw artist. Earp had seen Levy in action in Deadwood and knew him to have ice water in his veins. Earp bet on Levy — and won.

The fight started when Harrison turned the corner and saw Levy step off the steps of the Dyer House and onto the muddy street. Harrison drew both guns and literally burned them up as he shot round after round at Levy.

Calmly, Levy pulled his single Colts .44 laid it on his left arm, sighted along the barrel and pulled the trigger. One round, just above the belt buckle, and Harrison was a loser — forever.

"Duck Bill" Hickok?

According to an indictment drawn for murder in Gage County, Nebraska, July 13, 1861, James Butler Hickok — Wild Bill to you and me — was then called "Duck Bill" Hickok!

That is a fact. And, the story behind the indictment and the shooting is interesting, and one that Hickok fought over. As a matter of fact, Hickok killed over the story.

Young Hickok had been mauled by a bear while driving stage for the Overland Company on the Sante Fe Trail. The company, knowing he was a top hand with horses, but crippled in their employ, sent him to Rock Creek, Nebraska, to handle horses while he recovered. He was then twenty-two years old, and the fame as a gunfighter-gambler-scout had not yet been achieved.

He was a handsome man, tall, rawboned, and graceful. He had been described by Mrs. George Armstrong Custer who once said, "I do not recall anything finer in the way of physical perfection than Mr. Hickok when he swung himself lightly from his saddle, and with graceful, swaying step, squarely set shoulders, and well poised head, approached our tent for orders."

While that tribute to Hickok's looks was written eight years after Hickok's indictment for murder in Nebraska, it gives an insight into the kind of man he was, and in 1861 he was just becoming a bit of a dandy, letting his hair grow long, struggling to affect the sweeping and curved handlebar moustache of the times. But, he had one facial characteristic that stood out.

He had a long Roman nose, curving, hawklike down to meet a lantern jaw and chin that nearly met his nose. For that reason, young Bill Hickok's new boss at the Rock Creek stage named him, when he first laid eyes on him, as "Duck Bill."

The stage station manager, Dave McCanles did not know it, but that nickname and his constant badgering of the young frontiersman sealed his own death warrant.

Two months after Hickok, or "Duck Bill" as McCanles called him, arrived at Rock Creek, McCanles was fired. A new man was placed in charge of the stage station, and one who did not call Hickok names, but liked him and made him manager of the station.

When McCanles came back to Rock Creek, he threatened the men working there and brought Jim Woods and Jim Gordon with him to back up his bullying act. "Duck Bill" killed all three in a wild gunfight.

He drilled McCanles with a rifle as he stepped into the station. Then, carrying two Colts, he slipped out a side door and with three well placed shots, resolved the situation in less than five minutes.

Some called it a cold blooded killing, and so an indictment was delivered to him by Sheriff E.B. Hendee of Gage County. His name was spelled "Duch Bill," meaning a poor speller had just left off the "k" in duck. But, the judge gave Hickok his freedom based upon the fact that all three men who had tried to take by force things that belonged to the Overland Company were armed, and young "Duch" was merely defending himself.

Years later Hickok was to recall the incident as he stood before Reverend W.F. Warren, the minister of the Methodist Episcopal Church in Cheyenne on March 5, 1876, and married the leading female equestrian in America — Agnes Lake Thatcher. One hundred and fifty days later, "Wild Bill" was killed by Jack McCall in Saloon No. 10 in Deadwood holding the famous "Deadman's Hand:" an Ace of Spades, an Ace of Clubs, a Queen of Hearts, and both black eights.

Flat Nose, Big Nose, Kid — Curry?

Modern western writers seem to have a lot of trouble sorting out Curry from Currie and Big Nose George from Flat Nose George. So, let us end the mix-up right here and now by starting with the one common denominator they all had — all were badmen, outlaws, or killers.

First, Flat Nose George Curry (sometimes spelled Currie) was one of the original users of The Hole In The Wall hideout, from which he and his gang of five or six men made a number of forays between 1894 and 1900. Once, they held up the general store at Wolton in June, 1898. It was not exactly a big time deal, and they came away with about $300 worth of goods and cash.

At first, Harvey Logan took up with Flat Nose. But he got tired of the small time activities, and with the kind of killing instinct he had, bigger robberies had to be in the offing, and he actively sought them. He took the name of Curry, some say because he liked Flat Nose.

In any event, Harvey Logan and two of his three brothers died violent deaths in their careers as gunmen, killers, and outlaws. After an abortive attempt to hold up a bank in Belle Fourche, Harvey rode south into the Brown's Hole region in the southwest Wyoming-Colorado borderland and joined with Butch Cassidy. A younger man rode with him, the Sundance Kid, whose real name was Harry Lonabaugh.

By now, Logan was known as Kid Curry to all, and his record for killings was viscious, one of which had to do with him nearly stomping a man to death, and then standing over the man, who was twice his age, and pumping him full of Colts .44 holes.

He was part of the Cassidy inspired Wilcox Train Robbery of June 2, 1899, the loot from which amounted to well over $30,000. Part of the gang went north, and fought a gun battle with a posse north of Casper during which Sheriff Hazen of Douglas took a bullet in his chest that killed him a week later.

Just prior to that, Curry's brother Johnny had been killed by an irate husband, and following the Wilcox job, Lonny Logan died in his aunt's front yard on February 2, 1900, as he tried to shoot it out with a posse.

Once all the brothers had died, Kid Curry trailed down the man who killed his brother Johnny up in Montana, and finished him off a few weeks after he and Cassidy and the Sundance Kid successfully knocked off the train at Malta for $85,000.

Later, Kid Curry was caught in Tennessee and jailed. He escaped by using the wire from a broom handle as a small noose with which he roped a guard and took off. He was finally captured, but turned his .44 on himself rather than spend time in jail.

That was 1903, and yet the story persists that he was wounded near Kaycee that same year, and wound up at Thermopolis where Dr. Julius A. Schulke treated him twice before saying he would die.

The third party to this story was Big Nose George Parrott. He was a successful road agent in the Black Hills area in 1876-77. But, when he tried to pull off a train job near Medicine Bow, he failed, only to have a couple of lawmen trail him and his gang near Elk Mountain. Both lawmen were ambushed, and Big Nose fled to Montana. One of the members of the gang was caught, and a mad mob took him from the law at Carbon and lynched him. He was Dutch Charlie.

Later, Big Nose was captured, and when he passed through Carbon, the same gang waylaid Carbon County Sheriff Rankin and tried to lynch Big Nose, too. But even though they used the same telegraph pole, they did not get the job done, and relented. So, Big Nose got to go to Rawlins where he was jailed.

Even then, a lynch mob took him out of jail and tried to lynch him again, but failed again.

Justice seemed too slow to all those folks along the Union Pacific tracks, and their hatred for anyone who had anything to do with the murder of the two Carbon lawmen who had been killed by the Big Nose Parrott gang was amply demonstrated in their repeated attempts to speed justice up and do away with Big Nose.

They got the job done March 22, 1881. And after Big Nose had been on display long enough, Dr. John E. Osborne cut him down and then skinned off parts of his hide making a covering for a pair of favorite shoes and his medical bag.

It is interesting to note that Dr. Osborne was Governor of

Wyoming from January 2, 1893, to January 7, 1895, and served one term as U.S. Congressman from Wyoming in 1896. I wonder if his campaign slogan was — "I'll Skin My Opponent at the Next Election!"

Cattle Kate

Trying to recover their losses from three disasterous years of severe winters, floods in the spring, and droughts in the summer, large Wyoming cow outfits were also nagged by an army of small rustlers who constantly chipped away at the large and defenseless herds of cattle owned by the big cowmen.

Finally, in desperation, because of the lax court system — either the judges were too lenient or the juries could not make up their minds about the rustlers brought before the bar of justice — the large cowmen hired their own range detectives or gunmen and hunted down the rustlers and handed down their own justice — frontier style.

This meant a hanging bee, or a necktie party.

One such occurrence, which was given wide attention, was the lynching of Cattle Kate and Jim Averell a few miles south and west of Casper on July 20, 1889.

She used the name of Kate Maxwell, but Cattle Kate's real name was Ella Watson, and she had been born twenty-eight years before her untimely demise in Kansas. Her father said she came West and worked along the Union Pacific as an actress, but sources closer to her said she was a dance hall queen and worked for Jim Averell.

Averell said he was a homesteader, but the truth is he ran a saloon and what passed for a ranch on the Sweetwater river. For a period of time cattle had been rustled, delivered to Averell who "sold" them, or at least gave Kate a bill of sale for them, then the cows were rebranded and turned loose in Kate's large fenced-in pasture. Then, they were pushed north into Montana and sold.

Both Jim and Kate hated the large outfits, and Jim wrote letters to the editor of the *Casper Weekly Mail* from time-to-time, damning the big cowmen as land hogs, water thiefs, and worse.

There seems to be no question that the cattle that Kate had in her pasture were stolen. The question was — how to prove it? This was virtually impossible, and besides using Kate, Averell could hide his actions behind the skirts of a woman. This made it doubly tough on honest cowmen trying to get their cattle back.

Thus, on the morning of July 20, 1889, seven determined ranchers rode up to Kate's place, cut the wire in her pasture, and turned the cattle out. They put her in a wagon and told her they were going to take her to Rawlins.

Then they drove over to Jim's place, drew their guns down on him, and told him the six shooters were the warrant for his arrest. They made him get into the wagon with Kate and drove off toward Spring Creek canyon.

There both Kate and Jim were hanged from the limb of a scrub pine tree. Thirty hours later, the bodies were removed by county officers from Casper.

Three months later in Rawlins, a grand jury failed to find a "true bill" against the men who carried out the hanging, and they were turned loose. Within a few years, four of the seven died violet deaths and another died of a rare disease. Thus, justice was served in the end — and at the same time, cattle rustling in that part of Wyoming came to a standstill.

Cattle Kate is the only woman in Wyoming history to die at the hands of a lynching party. The ironic part is it happened in the first territory and state to give women equal suffrage!

Part Six
Colorful Characters

Doctor Barber Versus Doctor Osborne

Including territorial governors, Wyoming has had a total of thirty-seven governors since April 15, 1869. Of those, a large number have been lawyers, merchants, stockmen and ex-soldiers. One was a dentist, and two were doctors of medicine.

The last two, Dr. Amos W. Barber and Dr. John Eugene Osborne were of the same period in time, and one followed the other into office.

Dr. Barber had come to Wyoming via Pennsylvania and had been a staff physician at the Pennsylvania Hospital in 1883. He made his way to Wyoming as the Doctor in charge of the military hospital at Fort Fetterman. During his medical-military career he had campaigned with General Crook in Arizona, and wound up at Fort Russell, now known as Fort Warren, or better yet, Warren Air Base.

He practiced medicine in Cheyenne, became active in Republican party politics and was elected as the first secretary of state in 1890. When the first governor, Francis E. Warren, resigned to accept his new post as U.S. Senator from Wyoming, Dr. Barber became acting governor until a new election was held in 1892, with the newly elected man, John E. Osborne, another doctor, taking office January 2, 1893.

Dr. Osborne, three years older than Dr. Barber, was from Vermont and had taken his medical education at the University of Vermont and then came to Rawlins in the mid-1880s where he carried on his medical practice, was a Union Pacific Railroad doctor, opened a retail and wholesale drug business, and got into politics on the Democratic side of the aisle in 1883.

Dr. Osborne was also a sheepman of some note in the Rawlins

area, served as second mayor of Rawlins, and was the man who covered his medical bag with the skin from the lynched killer, Big Nose George Parrott.

As you look back on it, these two men — uniquely enough the only two medical doctors to become governors of Wyoming at almost identical years — seemed as if they were headed at one another on a collision course.

Neither was particularly fond of the other. One was a Democrat, one a Republican. And when Governor Francis E. Warren resigned, Dr. Barber became the governor in his place until Dr. Osborne was elected to fill the post in 1892.

Barber put in a tough two years having inherited the Johnson County War and all the attendent problems coming from that episode, and Dr. Osborne had just won a tough election beating Edward A. Ivinson, a Laramie banker, by 9,290 votes to 7,509. The Populists landed some offices that year, too.

And the Senate of the State was controlled by a hostile Republican majority. The Populists by virtue of having enough to control the House, whose margin between Republican and Democrat was slim, left Dr. Osborne in a very tough spot.

Then, he got to thinking the Republicans were not going to proclaim him governor, and he tried to storm the office — take it by force. In fact, they had a fist fight, and Dr. Barber held him at bay by winning. Finally, one night in December, he had a small boy crawl along the ledge to the governor's office, crawl through the window, and open the door from the inside. Then, Dr. Osborne took over the office and barricaded it until he was assured he would be officially declared governor by the canvassing board, which had been held up by a November blizzard.

In any event, the two doctors sure put on a full-fledged situation comedy act for all Wyoming to see and hear about.

One of the funny stories about Dr. Barber happened when he was in the Army at Fort Fetterman and a hard case cowboy came in to see him. He said, "I understand you clean teeth. I want a job done."

Barber told him he was a doctor, not a dentist, but could prescribe some good dental powder. The hard case got indignant, pulled a gun on Dr. Barber and told him either clean them, or get shot.

The upshot of it was that Dr. Barber cleaned the teeth with his own toothbrush, charged the man $5, and both were satisfied.

Big Phil — The Cannibal

In the years I have lived in Wyoming and read about the West, or visited with men and women who have lived here all their lives, I guess about as bizarre a tale as I have ever heard was about Phil Gardner, a huge mountain man who hailed from Philadelphia.

He was supposed to have become a cannibal.

Now, I cannot prove it. But, what I can do is tell you some of the stories about him and then let you make up your own mind.

Just about the first reference to him was when he was carrying dispatches from old Fort Laramie in southeastern Wyoming up to General Harney at Bismarck, North Dakota. That would be around 1855. Gardner had been living with a band of Arapaho Indians, had married into the group, and they thought he had come from the moon. He was big — nearly seven feet tall, and covered in buckskin, completely bearded with long hair and a fierce countenance; anyone at first might have thought he came from a strange race of men not to be found on this planet.

In any event, along with an Indian guide, Phil had carried a military message through a blinding blizzard from Fort Laramie up into North Dakota. Arriving several days after the time figured for his arrival, Phil came in alone. When asked where his Indian guide was, Phil threw down a frozen leg, which, according to the reports, had been gnawed upon. Phil told them the Indian tried to kill him in the blizzard, but he reversed the tables and got the guide first. Then, because they were starving, Phil said he ate the troublemaker. The leg he had carried along for provisions on the trail.

When that story circulated the countryside, no man would scout or walk the lonely trails with Big Phil whose title had now changed from Big Phil the Mountain Man, to Big Phil the Cannibal.

A few years later, he wintered in South Park, Colorado, near Kit Carson and a crew of fur trappers. Carson had heard the tale about Gardner and would not let him winter with him.

It was a particularly tough winter, and when the spring thaw finally did come, Carson sent a fellow named Jones to Phil's camp to see how he had come through the trying spell, when game was very, very scarce.

When Jones returned, he told Carson that Phil looked plumb good. Had wintered just fine, Jones said. Only one thing, Jones recounted, Phil's Arapaho wife was gone. Everything she owned was still there, but Jones said she had disappeared, and Phil would not tell him where.

Of course, they said he killed and ate her. But that is another unfounded story about Phil.

He finally fell heir to a noose of rawhide up in Virginia City in the 1870s where he was hanged for a badman. But until the day he died, the rumor persisted that Phil Gardner would rather eat people than beef. True or not, it is a bizzare tale coming out of Wyoming's colorful past.

The "Mortal Ruin"

Somehwere else I wrote about "lords and lordlings" who came out West, invested in land and cattle, and for a time controlled sections of land and helped direct the future of Wyoming.

Many of them came from Great Britain. One was a young fellow named Moreton Frewin who had been raised in Sussex county in England and was a landed gentleman. He and his brother Richard left Fort Washakie in 1876, crossed over the southern end of the Big Horn Mountains in the dead of winter, using a herd of buffalo to tromp down the deep snow ahead of them, then dropped down onto the Powder River country near where Kaycee is now.

When those two young Englishmen saw the vast country stretched out before them, they decided right then and there that this was to be their home. Moreton, leaving his brother behind, raced back to England, made a dozen impassioned pleas to his friends — mostly lords, earls, barons, and a duke or two — and raised thousands of English pounds to form the Powder River Ranche Company, Ltd. He bought out the 76 brand, and before long was rounding up 40,000 head of cattle on a spread about ninety miles long and thirty miles wide.

How this young fellow found the time, I do not know, but he went to New York, courted a Union League member's daughter, and married her. He then put her on the Union Pacific, stopped off at Rock River, and together with his wife's French maid and his English butler, struck off across country in his own stagecoach to come back to his log cabin castle he had erected near Sussex, Wyoming Territory, which he named after his birthplace.

His newly constructed home was the marvel of the country-side, as it was several stories high, had one main room with two enormous fireplaces, and the room was well over forty feet long, with a musicians' gallery above a sort of mezzanine lobby where soft violins helped Moreton, his bride, and their guests in 1880 to enjoy their evening repast. Naturally, the home was called "Frewin's Castle," and it stood there for many years.

As it turned out, his bride's sister had married Lord Randolph Churchill a year or two before, so when young Winston was born, his Uncle Moreton was a Wyoming rancher; thus, Winston Churchill not only had an American for a mother, but a Wyoming rancher for an uncle.

Uncle Moreton was some kind of a promoter. When the terrible winter of 1886 nearly struck the death knell to the entire cattle industry, Moreton was busy in International Falls, Minnesota, trying to build a place to freeze his beef for shipment via Great Lakes steamer, down the St. Lawrence and thence to England. He did build a refrigeration plant on the Summit between Laramie and Cheyenne. Uncle Moreton worked and worried trying to save his beloved 76 Ranch, but to no avail. Everything he put into it along with the Earl of Dunraven, and a number of other lords, went down the drain so that in the end, Uncle Moreton was known to his friends not as Moreton Frewin, but as "The Mortal Ruin."

Trader and Magician

Before I tell this story, I must be honest enough to say that I do not know if it is really true. Still, many of the facts are present and so, it bears repeating as one of the truly interesting Wyoming legends, which have not had enough said nor written about them.

For a period of five or six years, there was a trader in the vicinity of Reshaw's Bridge, which was located three miles east of Casper, who made his living off of trading items emigrants threw away. He in turn traded these discarded items to Indians for beaver pelts, buffalo robes, and gold, which they brought in from the Black Hills region.

The Indians knew where he got his barter, but since they needed iron that had been made into arrowheads, wanted old muskets repaired and other items such as cloth, trinkets, beads, and so forth, they continued to trade with Old Will, as he was called.

In the late 1850s they cornered him and demanded firewater, new guns, and ammunition, or they would cease trading with him. Knowing that they would kill white people with the weapons, and even if they did not have the guns and ammunition, whiskey would craze them into acts of violence, Old Will refused to meet their demands.

This went on for a spell, and while his trade did fall off some, he managed to keep his head above water. Then, Lieutenant Colonel Phillip St. George Cooke, commanding officer of the U.S. 2nd Dragoons, came through what is now Casper en route to quell any trouble that might be on the horizon in the Mormon War out in Utah Territory in 1857. With him was a surgeon named Edward N. Covey.

In visiting with Surgeon Covey, Old Will learned of the miracle of chloroform while watching the surgeon take a man's hand off.

That night, just before he went to sleep, Old Will devised a plan that would hold off the pesky Indians and in the morning told Surgeon Covey about it. The medical officer thought it a priceless idea and gave Old Will enough chloroform to hold him for a long spell.

Thus, in late October 1857, after the long column of dragoons had pushed through, the Indians arrived at Old Will's cabin and demanded guns, ammunition, and whiskey. Will told them he had magic powers from above, and if they did not leave him alone and quit threatening him, he had the power to kill, and then bring back that dead person to life, if he so desired! This was a new one. And most of the Indians respected it — all except a tough young war chief. Will finally told him he would use his power on him, if he were willing to take the risk.

No. But, the warrior said he had a dog he could preform his magic on. So, a large mongrel dog was taken inside of Will's cabin, where the trader secretly gave him a large dose of chloroform.

Then, he appeared before the Indians, carrying in his arms an apparently lifeless dog whose eyes were wide open, his tail hanging limp and his tongue lolling out of his open mouth.

After a half hour, with the Indians becoming impatient, Will said he would bring the dog back to life. But the mutt was really out. Remembering that the surgeon said a pin prick might cause a jerk, Will jabbed him with his belt knife, but the pup refused to react. Now, Will got a little worried as the Indians and the beligerant young war chief began to crowd him saying, "Bring the dog back to life!"

In desperation, Will took his hand ax and began to chop away at the dog's tail beginning at the tip. When he got to the place where the tail joined the dog, old dog came to, and howling loudly, sailed through the fire and out of camp!

So, Will became a person around whom the Indians walked carefully for many a year — not the least of which was the not-so-tough war chief.

The Rain Maker

I have read a hundred stories about men who could really turn on the faucet and make it rain, but never met one. That is, unless you count an old Shoshore Indian I watched stop rain from falling on a Sun Dance at Fort Washakie when I was a kid.

The medicine man was called out when the thunder heads began to build up. The audience was told that it was bad luck to have a sun dance spoiled by rain. Anyway, the medicine man stomped up and down for about five minutes, showing off his finery and kicking up a choking cloud of dust. Finally, he said the right words, and sliced the heavens in two with the eagle wing baton he carried. And, so help me, it did not rain.

Be that as it may, fellows who could make it rain were common near the turn of the century, and one of them came to Casper to make it rain. He was Frank Melbourn, and he made his home in Canton, Ohio. Casper residents and ranchers actually sent him a contract, and he arrived on the F.E. and M.V. Railroad (Fremont, Elkhorn and Missouri Valley R.R.) on August 6, 1891.

He had a glorious machine, which he claimed could bring rain in any amount. Only thing — no one was allowed to see his mechanical rainmaker! That was his invention, and he fully intended upon keeping it to himself!

Believe it or not, he did produce a shower the very next day. While it was not exactly a downpour, it did shower. Still, it was not enough to do the countryside any good, as it had been one of those years in which waterholes, creeks, and springs had simply dried up, and the whole prairie for miles around was dry as popcorn.

The following week, after circulating around town and receiving applause from those convinced he could bring on a downpour, Melbourn set up his rig and worked feverishly at making rain. No one could see what he was actually doing, since he hid everything behind a regular canvas castle. But everyone knew he was inside due to the noise pouring forth, and the blinding flashes of light intermittently occurring from behind the canvas wall.

Only a few drops fell, and while everyone else was unhappy with the results, Melbourn's excuse was that he wanted to see the baseball game that afternoon, and did not want to rain it out!

Anyway, he did try once again and worked the better part of twenty-four hours. When he saw that clouds were rolling up, he turned the machine off, but no rain came, and he left Casper quickly.

He traveled to Cheyenne where they were also in the midst of a drought and felt any moisture at all was better than not giving Melbourn an honest chance. He tried twice in Cheyenne, and a heavy rain fell both times.

The following summer, Cheyenne sent for Melbourn again, convinced the Ohioan was the answer to their prayers. This time, he was allowed to perch along with his machine inside the capitol dome of the State Capitol Building. After two days of working his machine, one writer said, "There was a heavy rain on Horse Creek, a light rain in Rawlins, and a fairly good downpour at Uva, but none in Cheyenne. Melbourn claimed the credit for these rains, but the people refused to pay him for his efforts, and he packed his machine and went to Kansas where the people were in great distress on account of a lack of moisture."

Melbourn, it is said, made a lot of money in Kansas, but we learned later most of the crops failed due to the lack of rain!

In any event, as far as it is known, Melbourn did not come back to Casper — nor, for that matter, to Cheyenne.

Diamonds Are For Nell

When Casper, as a city, was about six or seven years old in 1894, a dentist and an optician arrived in town from the Big Horn Basin. They were traveling and selling their services as they went along.

Dr. Will Frackelton who was to be a dentist in the Sheridan area for many years to come was one of the two traveling doctors. When spring had come in 1894, he and a Quaker optician had bought a team of Morgan horses and headed over the Big Horns for the Basin area to visit and examine eyes and teeth in hopes of repairing their fortunes.

After a good many mishaps, one of which was being involved with the Butch Cassidy gang near where Thermopolis is now located, they wound up in Casper in mid-July.

The Cassidy incident occurred as they were preparing to cross over the mountains to Lost Cabin, and they spent a night at a road ranch near the northern end of the Wind River Canyon. Only Dr. Frackelton's keen ability to handle a six shooter had saved them from being robbed of their hard earned savings. He was a good shot and proved it to the gang in an exhibition of shooting. That plus the fact that they left the road ranch at midnight and drove to Lost Cabin saved them from being overpowered and their earnings lifted.

When they got to Casper the two enterprising young men found that the town's only newspaper, *The Derrick*, had already gone to press and it was too late to announce they were ready for eye and teeth examinations at the Grand Central Hotel. It would be a whole week before the paper went to press again.

So, they printed a handbill and invited everyone in Casper to a dance at their expense to be followed by a free oyster supper. The dance was an immediate success, and the oyster supper was even more successful.

Thus, the next morning the first customer to visit the dentist was a very well-dressed lady, bedecked with jewels and dressed in the highest of fashion. This was the famed Poker Nell, a lady with a reputation for loving that particular game, playing with anyone, and best of all if the sky was the limit.

Dr. Frackelton said later on it was the oddest and yet, the best dental job he ever performed in fifty years of practice in the West.

Her problem? Well, nothing that really bothered her. Her teeth were in good shape, but she wanted him to set two perfectly matched half carat diamonds in her two front teeth.

She told him a dentist in Kansas City had given her the high hat, said it was not ethical to do it, but hoped way out here in Wyoming, he would forget ethics and do the job.

She said she wanted to show the ladies in Casper a thing or two. He said, "Yeah! And the boys, too. Because if I set those diamonds in your front teeth, the boys will be so busy watching your teeth when you smile, they won't watch the deal too close."

Anyway, he did set the diamonds in her teeth and to her dying day, Poker Nell — or, rather, Diamond Nell — carried them to her grave.

The Captain from Scotland

Of all the Europeans who came West, one of my favorites was Captain William Drummond Stewart. The second son of Sir George, the seventeenth Lord of Grandtully and fifth Baronet of Murthly, William did not inherit the titles nor the land from his father, and so, he turned to the army, where he served under the Duke of Wellington as an officer in the Sixth Dragoon Guards and was in on the kill, so to speak, of Napolean at Waterloo. Five years after this, he became a captain in the Fifteenth King's Hussars, a cavalry outfit, and then he retired on half pay to see the world — and flee, as it were — from the arms of a clutching wife.

He came to America in 1832, and by 1833 had visited with William Clark, of Lewis and Clark fame at St. Louis, before leaving for the West — and ultimately what is now Wyoming. As a matter of fact, he visited William Henry Harrison, the old Indian fighter near Cincinnati, and for a fee agreed to take the elder Harrison's son, Dr. Benjamin Harrison to the West for his health, where it was hoped he could help get Dr. Harrison off liquor and "dry" him out.

Thus it was that the veteran of Waterloo passed through Wyoming, past where Fort Laramie was to be located, through Casper, and on to Daniel in 1833 with forty men and a hundred and twenty pack mules loaded with trade goods on his way to a Green River Rendezvous, which took place July 5, 1833.

Stewart liked what he saw. He loved the Indians and all their colorful trappings, enjoyed meeting and visiting with the leather-clad mountain men, and most of all, fell in love with the towering and vast range of Wind River Mountains.

While I do not remember whether he helped cure the Dr. Harrison whose father went on to become the ninth President of the United States, I do know that the Rendezvous of 1833 was the first of ten more Rocky Mountain meetings that Stewart attended before he went back to his gloomy castle Murthly to assume his titles, since his elder brother died and being next in line, he was now a lord in his full birthright.

But before he went back to Scotland, he made his last trip west up the North Platte and this time, since he had money from his inheritance, he did his trip real justice. He took an artist named Alfred Jacob Miller with him, to record the fabulous country, and those paintings and line drawings were destined to become world famous. Also, Sir William took sixty men with him, a valet, two extra servants, and what is said to have been a remarkable tent which was red crimson in color and fourteen feet square. But best of all, the tent was furnished inside like his London apartment, complete with the best of wines and gourmet foods.

Yes, sir! The captain from Scotland loved this country, and believe it or not, named what we call Fremont Lake, Stewart Lake, and the New Fork Lake, Drummond Lake, long before Fremont came west.

When Sir William went home, he took some Indains, some buffalo, and a mountain man home with him as well as a multitude of the paintings of Alfred Jacob Miller. The only thing that survived, except scattered writings and journals of Stewart's visits to Wyoming, are the famous paintings that have been gathered together at various places and museums in the country. They catch the enthusiasm of Stewart and surely show the love this gallant Scotsman had for Wyoming nearly 150 years ago.

Unusual Women

A city ordinance in Casper dated July 20, 1889, stated that, "It shall be unlawful for any woman to use any vile, profane or indecent language, or to act in a boisterous manner, or to smoke any cigar, cigarette or pipe on any street in Casper, and if any woman shall do any of the named, she shall be fined a sum of not less than $5 nor more than $25 and said ordinance shall be in effect on all seven days of the week from 7:00 A.M. until 10:00 P.M."

What happened between 10:00 P.M. and 7:00 A.M. really did not matter, because Casper was then a hell roarin' cowtown, and some of the gals who worked in the temples of evil were cigar, cigarette, pipe smoking ladies who could handle the roughest part of the King's English with the best bull whacker to drive twenty-four yoke of oxen up the Oregon Trail.

That was the reason for the law — which, of course, no longer exists today.

I always liked the story about Phatty Thomas, the "ne'r do well" who lived in Cheyenne, being asked by a pal of his in Deadwood in the winter of 1876 if he could corral a freight wagon full of stray cats. Seems Deadwood, as a new town full of freshly sawed, slab pinewood, drew pack rats and field mice like the Pied Piper himself was playing his pipe.

Phatty's pal suggested that a good mouser could draw as much as $5, maybe even $10 to help keep down the mouse and rat population.

Phatty went to work, and by scraping the bottom of Cheyenne's cat barrel came up with several hundred stray cats, and loading them aboard an old wagon he rented, headed up into the Black Hills with his freightload of felines.

Crated up, and with Phatty driving his two-horse team, the cats were on their way to the glory that was Deadwood at its best during the huge gold strike then wheelin', dealin', and findin' gold nuggets as big as eggs or gold dust filled every prospector's wildest dreams.

En route to the famed area, Phatty had an accident. His wagon tipped over near where Hill City is today. Miners, taking a day off their hard work there, were amazed as they saw cats streaking around the hills like they had been scalded, but threw in with Phatty and hunted them down.

A couple of hours later, and a half wagon of cats later, Phatty got underway again, but felt low as his cat load was now about half as big as it had been when he started out from Cheyenne. His hopes for a big killing in the cat money market had dimmed considerably.

It was only when he pulled into Deadwood that he saw how much his feline freight was appreciated, as every businessman tried to outbid the other for the mousers. But, the madames who ran the temples of evil outbid all the bankers, merchants, and cafe owners. They got all of the cats, and that, ladies and gentlemen, is how the name "cat house" came to be applied to temples of evil where painted ladies work.

Another story I always liked dealt with Chief Spotted Tail's wife, or squaw, whichever you prefer. Mrs. Spot, as she was called in the local Cheyenne press in the 1870s, frequently accompanied her treaty-making husband to Cheyenne as he met with Indian commissioners bent upon drawing some sort of treaty for the Black Hills.

Old Spot, his real name was Than-tag-a-liska, chief of the Brule Sioux, and a man who counted twenty-six coups, was a frequent visitor to the old McDaniels Theatre in Cheyenne. He loved to see the stage shows and was always ushered to a box seat accompanied by his wife.

There they took in the performances while licking ice cream cones.

Once, Mrs. Spot went out to buy more cones and was promptly arrested by the local Cheyenne police. They thought, because she wore a single strand of braided hair down her back, that it was a pigtail and that she was Chinese. At that precise moment, a Tong War between the six Kung Chows, the nine Ning Yungs, and the eight Josh Wongs in Cheyenne was in progress. It is said Old Spot nearly lifted the scalp of the local cop who figured Mrs. Spot was Chinese and tossed her into the local hoosegow!

One other story about a lady of great courage in Wyoming always tickled me. This one had a husband who could not keep away from the poker tables in the local gambling palace in Newcastle. No matter how many times he promised to break the habit, he was drawn by the click of chips and the riffle of cards back to the green, felt-covered tables and thus, kept his wife and kids in a state bordering upon complete destitution.

One evening, while on her way back to their modest abode, the lady saw her husband playing poker. She edged into the saloon and saw her husband's hand was a loser. Just then, at another table, a man drew his Colts .44 and turned it on the lamps hanging over the tables. Everyone hit the floor, except our heroine. While the room was plunged into darkness, she calmly swept off all the poker chips from the table into her apron, and silently made her way out the doorway.

The next morning, she turned up in the saloon and demanded payment with the saloon marked chips — and got it, too. This act cured her husband from ever playing poker again, and she was $3,000 richer!

Powell On the Green

High in the Wind River range of mountains in western Wyoming, the first trickle of water forms the Green River. Just one of many streams found in the towering granite peaks along the backbone of America, the Green becomes, as it wends its way out of the southwestern part of Wyoming, one of the major sources of water of the mighty Colorado River.

The Green River is the start of a long series of vast chasms cradling the Green before it joins the Colorado River and then, together, the water moves on down into the Grand Canyon and finally dumps its constant supply of water into the Gulf of California.

Sheer walls rose from the floors of the valleys through which the Green ran, and much of them are now filled with the waters of Flaming Gorge Reservoir and other waters now saved by government projects.

But in 1869, when Major John Wesley Powell set forth on his river expedition from the present site of Green River, Wyoming Territory, the trip was regarded by government officials with high interest. Others who looked on the venture saw it in light of madness, romance, and a waste of money — perhaps life, too.

Not so Powell — the one-armed veteran of the Civil War who had spent his early life studying what is now called geology.

Not a reckless man, Powell had served with distinction in the War Between the States, even though carried on the rolls as a deserter at the end of the war. This came about as a result of his wound, and the constant number of operations he had to undergo before finally losing his right arm just below the elbow. No medical record had been served up to the Army and thus, while he was recuperating from a third operation in 1864, he was described as a deserter until he got to correct the record.

Losing an arm is bad, but in the course of doing so, he became a close friend of General Grant, who was for a time, his commanding officer. This came to his good stead on several occasions when, after the war, he tried to get financial and governmental support to carry out his plan for surveying and exploring the Green and Colorado rivers. President Grant was always his helper and his friend.

In any event, Major Powell gathered his ten-man party on May 25, 1869, in Green River, and after eating their last meal at Jake Field's cafe, embarked in four boats on what was to turn out to be one of the great waterborne expeditions in American history.

Eighty-five days later, two boats carrying six men emerged at Rio Virgin. The great expedition was over. One boat had sunk and one was beached. One man quit long before the expedition entered the Grand Canyon. Another three men quit just three days before the end of the voyage. They just could not face the rugged rapids ahead of them.

In any event, Powell and the rest of the party were proclaimed national heroes, a tribute well deserved.

Jenny

Jenny hailed from London. Born there, she had married a man named Orphansent Fish. You see, Jenny's husband had been found on the shores of a Scottish loch, and thus named Orphan-Sent, and given the last name of Fish.

Together, this pair came to America in the service of a wealthy and titled Englishman. Fish was the gentleman's man and valet, and Jenny a servant, maid, and cook. Together, they were as fine a couple as ever came to old Wyoming.

Now it seems in 1884 that young Gilly Leigh, who was actually Baron of Leigh, Stoneleigh County, Warwick, England, was visiting Moreton Frewin, the uncle of Winston Churchill and the owner of the famed Powder River Ranch, Ltd., at Sussex, Wyoming.

That puts Sussex a few miles east of where Kaycee is today. That is the place where a practical and hard-fisted independent cowboy went to greet an Englishman, also titled who was visiting Frewin at his "Frewin's Castle" ranch. And, when the cowboy saw the Englishman, and the visitor from faraway England told him, "You may inform your marr-ster" that he was there, the cowboy promptly and acidly told him, "The son of a b---- ain't been born yet."

It is also the place where the spouse of a titled Englishman watching a horse cavort and buck around a corral with Horace Plunkett aboard, overhead one cowboy tell the other that they had given Horace a buckin' bronco. At that moment, Plunkett was bucked off. She said, "I say — what did he do?" The ranch cowboy said, "Bucked." "Really," she said, "I say. What could have happened had he broncoed, too?" Plunket was actually Sir Horace Curzon Plunkett, son of Edward, sixteenth Baron of Dunsey, Ireland, and his uncle at that time was Viceroy of India.

Getting back to Gilly Leigh. It seems he had gone picking posies while elk hunting one foggy morning, and as he leaned over to grasp a flower, lost his balance, and fell about 1,000 feet straight down to his death in the Ten Sleep Canyon.

No one could find his body for several days, until circling buzzards gave away his position, which was in the topmost branches of a towering cottonwood tree. Getting the body down, they packed it horseback to the Bay State Ranch, where Jenny and Orphansent worked. The ranch was over one hundred miles from Frewin's ranch and on the other side of the mountains.

So, what to do with the body was the next question. No mortician lived within two hundred miles, and the family of Leigh wanted the body shipped to England for a family burial. Heavy snow prevented movement of the body by wagon until the spring thaws. So, they did the next best thing, as Jenny recalled years later.

The body of young Leigh was laid out in the main room of the ranch which was empty all late fall, winter, and spring, as the absentee owners only visited summer and early fall.

Then with the body covered with a sheet, the front door was cracked open to keep the room cool. And there the Baron of Leigh laid all winter. Occasionally, Jenny, who stood only 4 feet 10 inches, would stop by and lift the sheet to see how "Mr. Leigh," as she called him, was doing.

She said it was not so bad that fall or that winter and up until early March. But when the first thaw hit, Jenny said, "Mr. Leigh got a bit high."

Oh, yes. Leigh finally was hauled to Cheyenne, nailed up in a coffin and shipped home. But not before Jenny and Orphansent spent the winter with Mr. Leigh at the mouth of Ten Sleep Canyon in 1884-1885.

Chisholm

All the Chisholms did not come up the Chisholm Trail. Not by a long shot, because there was one who turned out to be a newspaper reporter, and he came west out of Chicago in the spring of 1868 to report the news of the big gold strike on the Green River.

This would be James Chisholm, a bonny Scotsman with a wry sense of humor liberally sprinkled with the milk of human kindness and a sharp eye for detail. He was also a fine writer, although as far as I can find out, none of his stories got into the *Chicago Tribune*, the paper which hired him to go west.

Fact is, his writings turn up in his diary, and it is priceless. For instance, he remarked about women in the West in this vein, after having come out of the Wind River Valley on a cold day in the fall of 1868 to sit down to a hot supper of fish, beaver tail, potatoes, and turnips topped off with bullberry pie:

> In this country it is better I believe, to marry a Squaw than a white woman. They are more profitable. They have no expensive luxuries, and they can dress skins, catch your horses and do all kinds of work. They are docile and industrious, and their conversational powers are limited. The great drawback is that you have generally to marry a host of relations along with them.

The column he proposed to write was to be called, "A Ramble in the Far West." And, after taking the Union Pacific Railroad to Cheyenne, he stopped off there for a quick look at the raw frontier city, which was the capital of territorial Wyoming.

He wrote that he saw one shooting, three hangings, and a blizzard within twenty-four hours, and if that was not enough, he wound up a day or so later in a lean-to type of cabin west of Cheyenne where he got snowed in. He said about this experience that there were so many cracks in the walls, he felt damned lucky he had not been snowed out!

Back in Cheyenne, the blizzard hit again and after going without food for a half a day, he said he crossed the street in the face of the howling winds, got mixed up and had to spend twenty-four more hours in a tailor shop, sleeping and keeping warm among the bolts of cloth until the wind died down. Then — another gunfight — and his caustic remark was that he was just a step from snowballs to pistol balls.

Over in the Wind River Valley, he went out with a hunter and later asking about hostile Indians who were on the prowl, he told a friend that he had not lost any Injuns, and that it was no part of his program to look for them!

James Chisholm did catch the flavor and the hospitality of the West, and I like the way he described this country when he said, "I have discovered, among other things, what I call genuine hospitality. It is not merely that I have been comfortably housed and have lived the best of fare. It is not an ostentatious kindness which looks for an equivalent. There is a hospitality of the eye and the heart. One has not to fight his way into it, if he is frank and honest. The stranger is welcomed as an old friend." And that's how it was in Wyoming in 1868.

Part Seven
Wheels and Rails

The Stage Line and Express Routes

Today, when you hear titles like Gilmer, Salisbury & Patrick or, Russell, Majors and Wadell, you would probably guess that they were a firm of lawyers.

But during the rush to the Black Hills for "Gold — from the grass roots down," as Custer had reported in 1870, those strings of names implied freighting outfits, express companies, or stage lines.

They found, in Cheyenne, a city founded upon the very spirit of free enterprise and proud to enter into competition with any other city in the United States. So, many of them based their operations in Cheyenne, which became the major outfitting center for the rush into the Black Hills, over two hundred and fifty miles north.

Large amounts of supplies had to be freighted into the hills, and so the supplies were off-loaded from the energetic Union Pacific Railroad in Cheyenne, then reloaded and hauled into the hills for the mines, mercantile operators, and owners of hotels, gambling houses, and a whole host of other business houses springing up overnight.

People had to travel to the hills, and so the stage lines jumped into action and traveled day and night, winter, spring, summer, and fall over rolling hills, down steep narrow roads, and through Indian infested country to bring the gold-hungry mob to their bonanza.

Because the hills were tough to get out of during the winter, many of the mines waited until the spring to send out their gold dust. Thus, the spring clean-up brought not only gold by treasure box after treasure box out of the hills in the merry month of May, but also an abnormal amount of stagecoach holdup artists.

Some of the more famous robberies in the history of gold mining took place between Cheyenne and Deadwood. And, equally some of the most famous marshall and law officers policed the trail.

The cattle from Texas made their entrance into Cheyenne in big numbers during this period, too; and, believe you me, Cheyenne was booming and bursting at its seams. Every type of world adventurer graced Cheyenne's city streets — day and night. Famous hotels grew, bawdy houses flourished, and great internationally known artists appeared in the opera houses of Cheyenne.

The military found, in Camp Carlin, the major supply depot for this wide district embracing the military posts strung along the southern half of Wyoming, and millions of pounds of supplies poured into and out of Cheyenne. Further, Fort D.A. Russell housed anywhere from ten to fifteen companies of infantry and cavalry at all times.

Red men, cowboys, freighters, drovers, drivers, gunfighters, scouts, gamblers, painted ladies, politicians, speculators, soldiers, miners, and foreign titled gentlemen strolled the streets of Cheyenne.

It was an exciting time to live. And, Cheyenne lived it up, and continued to grow and grow and its title — The Magic City of the Plains — meant much more than the first city to have electric lights.

Just Before the U.P. Came To Wyoming

You know, it took an act of Congress and five major surveys before the Union Pacific Railroad got the go ahead to punch its way across the rolling plains and mountains of southern Wyoming.

Not many folks remember those facts. They have heard about how much land the U.P. got on each side of the rightaway, and how much money in terms of dollars and cents that company got in terms of subsidies as they built trackage on the plains, foothills, and mountains.

But, the fact remains, the War Department got smart in 1853 and included in its annual request from Congress enough money to send five separate survey teams from the Mississippi River to the Pacific Ocean before they decided, in Congress, which route would be best for a transcontinental railroad.

Jeff Davis was the Secretary of War in those days. Remember him? He later ran the Confederacy during the Civil War.

Anyway, he got survey crews headed out on the northern route, or above us in the Montana region today; along the Overland, Oregon, and Mormon trails, then called the Central Route; the Buffalo Trail, or through Colorado; the 35th parallel, or just south of the Colorado border; and the southern route through Texas.

They used the same Jeffersonian precedent of the Lewis and Clark era; that is, they made complete studies of the geology, ornithology, topography, botany, zoology, and anthropology on these surveys.

As a matter of fact, these surveys represented the first accurate and comprehensive look for Americans at the huge blank spot on their maps of what was the uncharted and mysterious West.

In Congress, it was not a question of whether a Pacific Railroad should be built, but which one should be built first. New

England wanted the northern route, the South wanted the southern route, and the politicians in the Midwest, naturally, the central route. The coming of the Civil War settled the issue for the South and, finally, the choice was made in the Railway Act of 1852 to use the Union Pacific from the Midwest and the Central Pacific from the West, and aim them at each other so they could meet.

The rest is history. But the fact remains that it took a fiery Southerner in the role of Secretary of War, Jeff Davis, to get the nation moving towards building a railroad, and if you ever get the chance to pour through one of the huge twelve volumes published in 1855-56 on the surveys, you will find interesting and new approaches to the history of the state we live in today.

Iron Horses in Natrona County

Owen Wister, the famous writer who wrote *The Virginian* and a whole host of other books, visited Casper twice in his life. The second time, he wrote some pungent remarks about the railway service.

He had been up in the Buffalo country visiting Fort McKinney and on July 3, a Friday, in 1891, he wrote the following:

> In train leaving Casper. I was much struck by our manner of departure just now, ten minutes late. The train hands were doing nothing. Merely sitting on the platform or leaning against the doors of the station. That is all they had been doing for fifteen minutes, and I looked out of the window and wondered just when, and owing to just what, we should leave Casper. A man said, "Well, let's get out of this town." Apparently the conductor. Another in blackened overalls rose. Apparently the engineer. He walked towards the head of the train, out of my sight, and immediately we began to move. Some parties in the baggage car just in front are firing at the telegraph poles. Six shots and not a hit. Now comes a jack rabbit. Four more. "I guess the rabbit's safe," a passenger observed in the car. Now it is 8:50, shooting ceased and stopping at Inez, and empty is the shell of a station among sagebrush, pronounced "Eins" by the employees. I've just heard of this sort of thing, but never before saw it.
>
> We stopped, but not for passengers, but to hunt jack rabbits. There is a greyhound on board, and with him the conductor, a brakeman with a six-shooter, and one or two passengers scouring the plain in search of some game while the train waits. If I had a Kodak camera with me, I'd take a picture of the train here and I'd entitle it, "Waiting for Jack Rabbits."

Wister, an easterner, was not prepared for what he got in the way of a ride on the F.E. and M.V.R.R. It was largely an unscheduled train and the Fremont, Elkhorn and Missouri Valley Railroad was all that Casper could boast of in those days.

Later on, Casper would get the Chicago and Northwestern and then the C.B. and Q.R.R., but up until then, it was ride the F.E. and M.V. or walk. Many preferred the latter.

When the old F.E. and M.V. arrived in Casper, there was so much shooting that passengers were afraid to get off, until the conductor assured them that the citizens of Casper were not savages and would not shoot them!

One story about railroads has always delighted me. Rail service was established between Casper and Lander on the Chicago and Northwestern on Wednesday, October 17, 1906. Lander valley folks came for miles to see the train and after the Lander Silver Cornet Band finished performing, and the various clubs and lodges were through with their manuevers, and the mayor had finished giving his speech, finally, a railroad executive mounted the cow-catcher and described the glory of railroads and that ended the celebration. The engineer, a red-faced Irishman, looked out of his cab and yelled, "Stand back, I'm goin' to turn her around!" The crowd stampeded and scattered out of the way, while all the rail-roaders laughed until their sides ached. Then the crowd under-stood. The train could not be turned around on a one-way track, and then realizing the humor of the situation, joined in on the joke, too. The whole town of Lander laughed.

The railroads were vital in the development of Casper and central Wyoming. Oil, cattle and sheep, mail, freight, and passen-gers were carried faithfully for many years by the F.E. and M.V., the C. & N.W., and the C.B. and Q. railroads until the automobile and truck, plus the airplane, cut deeply into their business. Now, they haul only freight. The gentle art of taking a train ride from Casper north, south, east, or west, it would seem, is a thing of the past. Too bad — it was a great way to travel. It was the *best* way to travel.

Freighters

Well, we have talked about cowboys, soldiers, Indians, doctors, gunmen, law officers, badmen, prospectors, and a whole host of others, but have not yet touched on the freighter.

I did mention something about them in another story entitled "Jerk Line," but that is not freighting using huge, slow moving bovine oxen yoked up to big, heavy, lumbering freight wagons.

Before we got railroads or roads out here there were only a couple of ways you could move your personal belongings from one place to another place. If you were on the move to gold in California, taking up with the Mormon religion in Utah, or looking for land in Oregon, you loaded all the things you owned inside a Conestoga or Studebaker prairie schooner and plowed out West.

Now, if you were stocking a military post and you were in the quartermaster section of the Army, you had to hire freighters to carry flour, salt, coffee, arms, ammunition, clothing, and other items needed by the soldiers.

Generally speaking, a freight outfit looked something like this along about 1866. No tents, no stoves, and only fires over buffalo chips were used by these hard working, sunbaked freighters.

Their fare was coffee, bisquits, beans and bacon on the trail. They carried a fifteen to eighteen foot leather whip, which was braided onto a three foot leather handle, or stock. With this they goaded or snapped the whip above the heads of seven to nine pairs of huge oxen yoked together and pulling a big wagon that was coupled to another wagon of the same size. You would haul about three tons of material in these big old-time moving vans.

The freighter, swinging his whip above the heads of the animals so that it cracked like the sound of a heavy caliber rifle, was king of the road. Many of these men became so proficient with this whip that they could knock the head off a rose at twenty feet, ninety-nine times out of a hundred, and few people crossed them on the dusty streets of frontier forts and towns — especially when they were carrying their whips with them, which was all of the time.

They were a breed apart, and as they marched alongside their patient oxen, they jumped in to help the infantry or cavalry escort when a battle with red men took place.

Don't forget, it was freighters who were on the wood detail at the Wagon Box fight when Red Cloud took his historic defeat up near Buffalo and Sheridan in 1866.

And the Army was glad to have them around — those hard working and leather tough freighters — who walked literally thousands of miles when Wyoming was new and there were not too many iron or asphalt trails in the Cowboy State.

MORMONS CROSSING THE PLAINS.

Heavenly Handcarts

Of all the different modes of travel out here in the West, the handcarts the Mormons used were certainly an unusual sort of transportation.

They were light for good reason. They had to be pulled, or pushed depending on the grade up and grade down a hill by human beings — not animals!

Further, very little metal was used in the construction. They had high wheels and really nothing more than a bow inside, which you could get inside of to pull them, a small six inch high side-board, and they were about six feet wide and the same size in length.

Since no mule, horse, jackass, or ox pulled these carts, they were pulled and pushed by a father and a mother, and helped out by the strongest kids in their litter.

When Brigham Young was at his highest peak he devised this idea; bring the converts to Mormonism from the faraway lands to New York; entrain them to Florence, Iowa, and then form handcart companies under the command of the same elder who usually came across the briny deep with the converts.

These companies, and I mean they were companies of anywhere from 60 to 600 people, were made up of father, mother, and the offspring. It was not unusual to find a family of parents and anywhere from six to ten children ranging in age from one month up to twenty-five years old herding their handcart along.

At first, they went according to plan. So many people to a handcart, each person limited to seventeen pounds of belongings, so much flour, meat, rice, salt, and other supplies. Then a wagon followed the handcart company with extra provisions and several men on horses, and usually some oxen being driven to Zion — Salt Lake, that is.

If an emigrant got to Fort Laramie by July 1, then he was usually in good shape for the rest of the trail. I am talking about the slow pace set, and the fact that early fall snowstorms could catch you, desecrate your outfit, and in the case of the tragic Donner Party, practically eliminate you.

So, the handcart companies were doing alright in 1856 until about the fourth or fifth, which arrived in Fort Laramie about the early part or middle of September. By that time, they had gone through enough death along the trail from exhaustion and from disease. Remember, these folks were straight from the power looms in England, from the coal mines in Wales, from the factories of Europe. They were not conditioned mountain men nor seasoned soldiers, and as far as that goes, neither were the captains of the companies.

The worst disaster that ever took place along the Oregon Trail happened just a few miles west of Casper — beginning in the Red Buttes region and carrying on to the Sun Ranch when in November 1856, the fourth and fifth handcart companies were caught in a snarling, freezing blizzard that left snow anywhere from eight to eighteen inches deep on the treeless prairies.

The suffering was immeasureable. We know from the records left and on file in Salt Lake City today, that over two hundred and fifty people died on that stretch of trail — from exhaustion, from starvation, from the bitter cold — and as many more were amputees the rest of their natural lives.

If there is any place on the Oregon Trail that deserves a monument to ill-advice, to unpreparedness, and also to bravery and to a dauntless folk — it is Martin's Cove, just the other side of the Sun Ranch, where over two hundred and fifty faithful Mormons died in the terrible blizzard of 1856.

Jerk Line

I got to talking with a fellow the other day and he told me that as often as he had heard the term "jerk line," he really did not know what it was. Actually, jerk line was a term used by early-day freighters hauling supplies in and around Wyoming driving big teams of horses or mules.

You know, freight into Wyoming has always posed a problem. Long before we had multiton transports roaring up and down well-maintained highways or trains crossing our state, necessaries and supplies to our communities had to be hauled by teams of horses or mules in lumbering, heavy-built wagons. Depending upon the weight of the load, the teams ran from six to twenty horses or

mules. And, because the driver had his hands filled with lines or reigns, his brake was a long-armed affair sticking up in the air beside him with a rope tied to it so that when he had to set the brakes, he "jerked" the rope while still handling his lines. Thus, the term "jerk line."

Sheep outfits hauled their wool to the railheads, and it was not unusual to see a big wagon or jerk line up front with a smaller wagon hitched on behind with eight or ten head of animals pulling 20,000 to 40,000 pounds of wool packed into 500 pound sacks. Sometimes, a twenty-horse team could be seen pulling 40,000 pounds of wool! (See photo) It could be supplies to a mine, or it could be an ore wagon going from the mouth of a mine, or a load of timber or wire for a fence.

In any event, these drivers had their hands full in more ways than one, if you will remember that there was no highway department in those days filling in bad spots on the road. If you bumped into a real bad place, you climbed down from your wagon seat, got a pick and shovel and just filled in the chuck hole yourself. Either that, or drive around it — thus creating a new curve in the ruts called by those who used them, a road.

Now, a jerk line also meant that the team was driven by one line that ran down the left hand side of the teams to the head pair, called the loaders. Each animal in a well-trained team knew where they were going and answered to movements from the jerk line and the yells the driver executed.

The best horse was the jerk horse, as he controlled the whole team. When the driver gave a steady pull on the line, he would go one way. If the driver jerked the line, the horse would go the other way. Usually, on a winding road, the point team would pull sideways to keep the wagons in the road, and if it was a real dangerous hill, the swing team would pull sideways, too — if the driver yelled, jerked the line or pulled it for them.

Starting out the wagon, the freight outfit with an eight-horse team looked like this: wheel teams next to the tongue, then the point team, followed by the swing team, and the leaders were always up front.

When a good driver with a good team came to town, just about everybody stepped to their doorways to watch the driver swing his big team in a U-turn in the middle of the main street so he could either unload or take on supplies at the local hardware store. Many a bet was made on which driver and team was best, and on a good holiday many teams would line up at the city limits and come charging down a dusty Wyoming main street, their driver yelling, sawing on the lines, and wheel his team in a complete turn and return to the starting point. Best time always won, and in that day and age a good six or eight horse team with a wagon hitched to them was an important holiday event and usually was the opening for the local rodeo to get underway. My grandfather, Fred Bragg, was very proud of his Belgian horse teams, and they nearly always carried the day for him in those golden days between 1880 and 1920, when the Bragg Belgium teams were about the best there was in Wyoming.

Luke Vorhees

If ever there was an unsung hero of Wyoming, it was Luke Vorhees. His career began with the Pike's Peak gold rush in 1859, and it finally drew to a close in Cheyenne in 1925 where he died at the age of ninety.

For sixty-five years he was successively a gold miner, a cowman, in the freighting business, the superintendent and partner of a stagecoach line, ran a telegraph line, owned a pony express service, built the first gas works in Cheyenne, ran an iron foundry, was the first territorial treasurer, put in a term as Laramie County Treasurer, and in 1913 was appointed by President Wilson as Receiver of Public Moneys and Disbursing Agent for the U.S. Land Offices in Cheyenne.

Larger than life, Vorhees had a dry sense of humor as evidenced by a favorite story he used to tell. Seems as though two cowboys were arrested in Cheyenne before there was a formal jail. They were placed by the marshall in a tent that had the word "JAIL" painted on it. The men, waking some hours later with massive hangovers, since they had been more than tipsy when arrested, found themselves in dire need of a cool refreshing drink of water. So, they picked up the tent and moved it several miles to the banks of Crow Creek where they satisfied their burning thirst. When the marshall finally located his jail, they told him that rather than be jail breakers, they just took the canvas jail with them to the creek. The marshall let them off with a warning.

Vorhees could be tough, too. It was said that several well-known bandits and killers had been let off with lenient fines once too often for his taste. When the two were captured for holding up one of the stagecoaches on the line Vorhees worked for, vigilantes took the men away from the marshall and hanged them. While Vorhees said he had nothing to do with it, there were others who swore that Vorhees was behind the hangings.

As a young gold miner, he was the man to first bring in a sizeable discovery on the Kootenai River in what is now Idaho. He actually built big fires along sandbars in the river to thaw the ice so he could pan for gold before the spring thaw produced a big rush. His take for one winter of work in the area was 200 ounces of gold dust.

Moving down to Salt Lake, he went to Texas and invested his gold dust in a herd of longhorns then trailed them back to Utah, where he sold them for a good profit. It was during this period that he turned up as one of those spectators who witnessed the driving of the golden spike at Promontory Point in 1869, which tied the Union Pacific to the Central Pacific Railroad.

With money in his jeans, he bought into the newly formed stage line being set up by Gilmer, Monroe, Salisbury, and Patrick at Cheyenne. He also became the superintendent of this line formally called the Cheyenne and Black Hills Stage, Express and Passenger Line. All he had to do was locate a practical route from Cheyenne to Deadwood, not to exceed three hundred miles, organize and equip stage stations every fifteen miles, and further, it was his responsibility for the safety of the passengers and the transport of gold bullion.

But, Vorhees was up to the job. He first ordered thirty, four-horse and six-horse Concord stagecoaches, then went out and bought 600 head of horses, and hired the best drivers he could find. He even set up a program where each team had its own particular harness.

Someone will write a book about Luke Vorhees one of these days. It was men like him that helped Wyoming become a state. When they do write that book, they will probably use one of Luke's typical statements, which ran like this: "A man likes to be a creator of circumstances, not altogether a creature of circumstances."

Part Eight
Places

"Justice" and the Ames Monument

The highest point on the Union Pacific Railroad as it crosses the nation is located 8,235 feet high between Cheyenne and Laramie, Wyoming. It was here, near the old railroad station of Sherman, that officials of the company decided to erect a huge monument to Oakes and Oliver Ames, the two brothers probably most responsible for the building of the railroad.

The granite monument was to be geometrical in shape, like a pyramid, sixty feet square on the ground and sixty feet high. It was built of granite, which came from a point about a half mile from the monument site.

A crew of nearly fifty men were employed in cutting the huge granite blocks, which were then hauled to the site. The work continued the best part of 1881 and 1882.

Once the monument had been dedicated, a local newspaperman in Laramie had been contacted by a patent medicine maker, who asked him to see to it that a large painted sign telling of the wonders of his medicine be slapped on the side of the monument. After all, the monument was the only broadside near Sherman on which a sign could be painted and read by a railroad passenger. When the news came out about this, it electrified the national press, who felt this sort of advertising was outrageous.

As it turned out, the newspaperman wrote the story about a sign being painted on the monument when, in fact, no sign had been put up at all. The national publicity was better anyway, and the patent medicine man got more than his share of national publicity.

The stunt however, served to arouse the curiosity of an Irish justice of the peace named Murphy in Laramie. He knew that sections of land in a checkerboard fashion had been granted by a grateful government to the railroad company for building their line. The alternating sections were still public lands.

Murphy decided to slip over to Cheyenne to find out the answer to the riddle. Sure enough. The Union Pacific built their monment on public lands, and with this information in his pocket, Murphy went to the public land office and filed on the section where the monument was located. He actually filed on that section as a homestead.

When he got back to Laramie, he sat right down and drafted a letter to the Union Pacific in Omaha saying, "I would be greatly obliged if you would take that pile of stone off my farm!"

Murphy's letter hit Omaha like a bolt of unwelcome lightning. A top-notch attorney was immediately dispatched to Laramie where he learned from Murphy what the asking price was for that section of land. Naturally, the price was sky high. Yet, the attorney knew a monument costing nearly $50,000 and weighing thousands of tons would be impossible to move.

Well, after much haggling back and forth, pressure of a political nature was brought to bear on the justice of peace. He was told that it could be construed as a conspiracy for a judge to take advantage of his neighbor — in this case, the railroad. If the judgment went the wrong way, impeachment proceedings might even be brought against Murphy, and everyone knows that if you are impeached, it could carry a sentence with it and worse — you could not vote in the future, or hold public office.

With visions of social disgrace staring at him, loss of work and, being branded a criminal, Murphy finally settled for two city lots.

He gave up his farm on Sherman Hill, kept his job, and the Union Pacific got back its Ames Monument — intact — and you can visit it today, high on top of Sherman Hill between Cheyenne and Laramie, Wyoming.

Fort Davy Crockett

Just about everybody knows that Davy Crockett was killed along with nearly two hundred defenders of the Alamo in what is now Texas on March 6, 1836. Crockett, a professional backwoodsman, fell alongside those brave Texans when Santa Anna assaulted the Alamo on that fatal day.

Crockett was popular with his contemporaries, that is the leather clad mountain men, traders, soldiers, and trappers. He was fearless, could play a fiddle, and as one said, "Had a heap a' courage."

Less than six months after Crockett was killed at the Alamo, a fur trading post was erected in Wyoming and named Fort Davy Crockett. Few folks in Wyoming know this fact, but Crockett's friends liked him so much they sought to perpetuate his memory in building this log and adobe fort on an elbow of the Green River in Brown's Hole, a few miles south of Rock Springs and Green River.

The fort was owned and run by three men — Phillip Thompson, William Craig, and a fellow named St. Clair. It was probably built in the late fall of 1836. The first official hunter employed to supply Fort Crockett with meat was Kit Carson, who worked there the winter of 1836-37.

The diaries of the early travelers report that the fort turned out to be a popular post with the Shoshone Indians and mountain men, like "Broken Hand" Fitzpatrick, Jim Bridger, Milton Sublette, and Joe Meek, who spent time at Fort Crockett, even wintering there. Using the fort as a base of operations, many of those early-day trappers slipped south into Navajo country trading their beaver skins for mules, horses, horse hair ropes and bridles, as well as the very popular Navajo blanket.

This blanket was first in priority. It was substantial, it was warm, waterproof, and usually had a pleasant pattern. Thus, it was highly thought of as an object of trade.

One early writer said that he suspected the trading parties were, in reality, "raiding parties." Be that as it may, after the mountain men made their swap, they would make a big swing east, coming back to Bent's Fort on the Arkansas, where the spoils were sold for the Missouri market. Then they would head back to Fort Crockett or other northern trading post adjacent to beaver country.

T.J. Farham wrote in 1839 that he had spent seven delightful days at Fort Davy Crockett. He said that the food supply was a might scarce and slim that August as the elk and buffalo ranged north of the fort in the summer months, returning to that area during the winter. So, according to Farnham, he dined along with others on "barking mutton" — just plain dog to you and me!

This fact did not upset Farnham as he went on to describe the overpowering scenery, the multitude of Shoshone Indians who had pitched their tepees around the fort, and the wonderful hospitality given him by his hosts who even let him sleep in their private quarters.

A few years later, when the beaver trade began to fall off, the fort was abandoned. It was too far off the Oregon Trail to supply emigrants, and so it died a natural death. Captain John C. Fremont noted the post to be in ruins when he passed it in 1844.

But the fact remains, Davy Crockett — immortalized by song, book, and movies — had a fort built and named after him over one hundred and forty years ago in Wyoming.

Suggs

About fifty miles west of Gillette, the little town of Arvada stands by the Powder River. It is also resting on the site of Suggs, Wyoming.

While lots of oil and coal movement has taken place around Suggs-Arvada, I would not publicize the area as an agricultural heaven.

Maybe sheep and cattle — but not crops.

One old-timer was asked how his hay crops would do? He said, "If I go over it real careful with a pair of sheep shears, and then rake it, real careful with a fine tooth comb, maybe, with lots of luck, I'll get about 160 acres to the ton!"

Before Arvada arrived on the scene, Suggs was a little gambling resort that grew when the old B. and M. Railroad was being built across northern Wyoming. Also, at the same time, due to the unrest resulting from the Johnson County War, a regiment of black cavalrymen was on manuevers in northern Wyoming during that period.

Those soldiers were named by the Indians "buffalo soldiers" because their hair was curly like that of the buffalo. It was a title the black soldiers carried with pride.

In any event, one day a number of black soldiers arrived in Suggs and got involved in a "gallopin' domino" game with one Jack Bell, and Ed Bennett, local gamblers.

Bell and Bennett were tough hombres. They wore their guns low, dealt cards fast, and handled the dice, or gallopin' ivories with equal dexterity.

In fact, as the buffalo soldiers found themselves soon fleeced of their hard earned pay, they began to think that Bell and Bennett had been playing with crooked dice. That called for an excursion into their gambling and drinking palace, and within minutes a small war was going full tilt.

The upshot of it was that two buffalo soldiers and their horses were killed. Ed Bennett was shot through both arms. So, there was only one hospital case — Bennett. Both soldiers and their respective horses represented the permanently disabled list. That called for an armistice, which is still in force today. Maybe that's why Arvada sleeps, not half as wild as it once was!

How Battle, Wyoming, Got Its Name

A good many Wyoming points of interest got their names from mountain men, or by some action that involved a mountain man. One such place in Carbon County is the town of Battle, Wyoming. Now a relic of the past, Battle was located near the Colorado-Wyoming border south of Saratoga and Encampment, Wyoming.

The story of the fight from which the town derived its name is not too well known, although it turns out that a two-day battle between hostile Indians and a brigade of fur trappers was fought here August 21-22, 1841.

The trappers led by Henry Fraeb, whose name appears in many early fur company journals, were attacked by a force of approximately five hundred Sioux and Cheyenne Indians at the southern end of the lush Saratoga Valley.

Upon seeing the Indians bearing down upon the brigade, Fraeb, or Frapp as he was called by his contemporaries, yelled, "Fort Up! Fort Up!" meaning each man was to kill his mule or horse after leading the animals in a circle. Then, with the animals on their sides, the mountain men could crouch down inside of the barricade of horse and mule flesh, thus forming a fort from which they could protect themselves while carrying on a defensive action against an attacking enemy.

Frapp had picked a smooth, rounded hill for his defensive position, thus the men had no choice but to follow his orders and "Fort Up!"

Jim Baker, another well-known beaver trapper, was a member of the Frapp trapping party and fought in the two-day battle. He lived to give a colorful account of the whole battle.

Baker said, years later, "After chusin' a round hill outen which we wuz to fight, we wuz surrounded by near five hundert them hostile red devils all wantin' our hosses, beaver plews and mules and women."

"Wal, we fought outen our dead animal fort and breastworks for two days and two nights," Baker continued. "They lost near 100 dead and wounded while we lost four dead and a couple wounded."

He said, "On more times than I like to remember, them 500 would charge right up to ten and fifteen paces of us. Yes, sir! We had us a right lively Battle!

"We finally won when they seed they hadn't a chanct to win, us with good rifles and them with bows and arrows and old smooth bore guns."

Before ending Baker told how Frapp was killed. "He wuz killed, but he never fell. Just sat braced up again a stump. So, we buried him right on the spot with $80 gold in his pocket."

Having lived with the Indians for a long time, mountain men often buried their friends with all their belongings, figuring that they could use good luck in the hereafter, or some pocket money wherever they were headed!

Baker told a story about Frapp, a St. Louis trapper of German descent, that bears repeating. Frapp had led a brigade of trappers into northern Wyoming, right in the heart of Blackfoot country. Here they built a headquarters lodge and concealed it so the Indians could not find it, or them; and they trapped the summer of 1839 for the highly sought after beaver pelt.

Baker recounted that one afternoon a violent electrical storm arose. The highly excitable Frapp, who at best Baker said, could hardly be understood because of his broken language, was inside the lodge when a bolt of lightning crashed into the ground near the doorway of the lodge killing one of the men named Gutherie.

Frapp rushed outside shouting, "Py Gott! Who did kill Guttery?"

A Kentucky born mountain man named Hawkins replied with his native drawl, "The Good Lord, I reckon'. He's a-firin' into camp!"

Henry's Fork Rendezvous: Ashley's First Rendezvous

About forty-five miles south of Green River and at a point on the banks of Henry's Fork, the very first fur trader rendezvous was held in 1825. A couple of years prior to that, William Ashley had tried to ascend the Missouri River, but had been beaten off by Indians. So, he turned right around and started his trading over South Pass, and down into the area just below Rock Springs and Green River known as Browns Hole and the stream now called Henry's Fork.

Ashley, a brigadier general in the militia of Missouri and its first lieutenant governor, was a good businessman. He determined that hauling his supplies to barter such a long distance from St. Louis called for a central place from which he could trade for the much sought after beaver plew — or skin. Thus, he choose for his first meeting in the summer of 1825 Henry's Fork, and the big event came off as planned.

Mountain men from all over assembled that summer. Jedediah Smith, whose middle name was Strong, and huge he was, came to trade. So did Broken Hand Fitzpatrick, Jim Bridger, Kit Carson, David Jackson for whom Jackson Hole got its name, Henry Fraeb, or Frapp as he was called, and many others.

A colorful lot, these men who did not care for the so-called civilized world, led a virtual savage way of life. Clad in buckskin, a fur cap for a hat, moccasins for shoes, a butcher or bowie knife at their sides, and a Hawken percussion rifle as their best friend, they traveled from the Mexican border to the Canadian border spending half their lives standing waist deep in ice cold streams setting traps for beaver.

So, when they got a chance to trade in their beaver plews for a new knife, more powder and lead, a blanket, and some beads and trinkets for their Indian wives along with some pop-skull, tangle

FIRST PRIZE
FORTY ROD

foot — whiskey to you and me — they did it willingly and with lots of excitement.

The rendezvous was, in a very real sense of the word, a Rocky Mountain carnival. There were foot races, wrestling matches, shooting contests, fist fights, knife duels, horse races, and above all — long drawn out and vigorous drinking contests. For these were men used to the solitary way of life.

Many times, their very lives depended upon stealth. How softly could they steal through the Blackfoot country more than once gave them another year on their lives.

So, when the time came to let loose — wound up as they were — they let go and really had a first-class fling.

Then, when they had traded in their otter, martin, fox, and beaver skins and filled their "possible" bags and loaded up on "necessaries," off they would go in search of a new watershed teaming with beaver.

This mode of life was to happen again and again until about 1843. Then beaver was no longer the big trade item. Silk hats replaced beaver hats.

But between 1825 and 1845, a twenty year period, the fur trapper and the fur trader met in areas like Henry's Fork and with an assortment of Shoshone, Ute, Crow, Sioux, Arapaho, Commanche, and Cheyenne Indians they held many a meeting, or the rendezvous. Sixteen of them were held inside Wyoming, near Green River, Pinedale, Fort Bridger, Lander, and Riverton, Wyoming. The others were held in what is now Idaho or Utah — within shootin' distance of Wyoming!

Rogers' Ladder

It took a local resident in the Sundance-Newcastle area to make the first successful climb of Devil's Tower. And he did it the most practical way he knew. He built a ladder up the side of the Tower.

Oh, it was not all the way to the top of the 1,200 foot rock tower, but it reared itself up 350 feet high and so, when William Rogers waved farwell to well over 2,000 people who had arrived to spend the long Fourth of July weekend in the Devil's Tower area in 1893, Rogers knew exactly what he was doing, and in less than two hours had planted Old Glory, our national ensign, smack on top of the sheer rock monolith.

For a month before the Fourth arrived, Rogers and his helper, William Ripley — no relation to Robert Ripley of "Believe It or Not" fame — had been working their way up the tower from the best climbing side. Then having found their way easily to within 350 feet of the top, they starting driving oak and ash pegs of about twenty-four to thirty inches in length into a vertical crack the rest of the way. This was followed by constructing a ladder of sorts to the pegs.

By now, publicity had built up regarding the climb, and the handbills scattered around the Black Hills announced there would be lots of dancing — day and night — fun and games, good meals, and hay and grain for all horses.

The dawn broke clear and fine, and at noon Rogers and Ripley started their climb. Two hours later, the flat was seen on one side of the tower, and in sight of thousands of people. The first successful ascent of the formidable tower was made first by Rogers, and then by Ripley.

A couple of years later, in 1895, Mrs. Rogers climbed the tower, too, and used the same ladder her husband had built, thus setting the record as the first woman to climb the tower.

Ten years later, President Teddy Roosevelt proclaimed it as the first National Monument, using the bill U.S. Senator Warren from Wyoming had introduced in the Senate in 1892, when the area near it had been named a U.S. Forest Reserve.

Up until Rogers' climb, the tower had not received a whole lot of publicity. As a matter of fact, it was not until 1875 when Colonel Richard Dodge described it as one of the most remarkable peaks in this or any country that the tower — called Bad Gods Tower by Indians, and thus named Devils Tower by white men — received publicity of its unique geologic features.

It was not until 1931 that the tower was scaled by normal alpine climbing techniques when the New York City Alpine Club, led by Fritz Weissner, scaled the sheer walls. They did it in four hours and forty-six minutes.

And you all remember when the part-time Black Hills mechanic and professional parachutist jumped on top of the tower from an old biplane in October of 1941, and then had to spend several days up there until a Dartmouth climber by the name of Jack Durrance was able to bring the scared Hopkins back down again. Goodyear Blimp and the U.S. Navy offered to bring Hopkins down — via blimp or helicopter — but Hopkins came down with Durrance blindfolded, it is said, because it was better he not see as they went over the side — he might have caused the whole party to fall! In any event Hopkins collected the $50 bet he had made that he could jump on top of the tower.

A mountain climbing teacher by the name of Walt Bailey used to give his "final" grades to his Casper College students on top of the tower. If the student could finish the climb, a passing grade was issued. On the other hand, I'd say it was the kind of class no one wanted to flunk!

The Occidental Hotel

I always got a kick out of stopping in Buffalo and slipping into the old Occidental Hotel. Oh, I know it is not really the same hotel where Owen Wister's "Virginian" stayed along with his friends McLean, Scorpio, and the rest. But it is nearly the same one, in that it was just rebuilt out of brick to take the place of the old log and native lumber, felled in the Big Horn Mountains nearby.

Still, on a quiet summer evening, if you have just finished reading *The Virginian*, and you step into the saloon and lobby and listen to the old-timers in their sharp, high-heeled boots, old battered Stetson hats tilted back, and rump worn Levi's — you kind of drift back to those by-gone days.

I always did think too much emphasis was given to Medicine Bow when most of the action took place from Casper north to Buffalo. And the center of action was the Occidental.

You know, the old hotel got its start right after the Custer Massacre. Charley Buell was cooking in his tent one day when some miners from up on Clear Creek asked if he would board them. He even cached some gold for them — placed it in a hole he had dug right underneath his bed — that was a safe place!

Next morning, he cooked up some flapjacks and fed them beans, bacon, and hardtack for the next several days.

It got to be a fact that Charley Buell could really take care of you, and one thing after another happened until he finally was persuaded to throw up a frame building in the new town of Buffalo. That was the beginning of the Occidental, a name by the way, adorning hotels all the way from the Sabine to the Milk River on the Texas Trail.

By 1880, the Occidental had served as saloon, cafe, hotel, court house, meeting hall, jury room, mortician parlor, wedding place, and many a fine ball and dance was held in and out of the main floor rooms. You even voted there, on occasion.

When Johnson County was formed, it was in the Occidental Hotel where the election of the newly formed county officers was held.

Once there was a gunfight that happened in the hotel, and if you were to read about it, you would say it was a lie. But one feller shot another feller one cold winter day point-blank. The bullet made its way clear through a big old overcoat, through a couple other coats and sweaters, a heavy suit of winter underwear, and finally got to his body where it barely got into his rib cage and dropped into his chest cavity. There are those who say that Arapaho Brown, he is the feller got shot by Red Angus, carried the bullet in his chest 'til the day he died. Oddly enough he died from another taste of lead poisoning.

Well, that's the way I heard it. And I never argue with those hombres up Buffalo way.

"Boom" Town — Casper

Over the years, Casper has enjoyed one type of boom or another. In the very early days, it was like a land boom with the westward rush of '49ers coming up the Oregon Trail. Then there were the cowmen pushing their four-legged charges north. When ranchers took hold of the land around Casper, and the town started to grow, there were also booms in cattle, sheep, oil, uranium, and other minerals.

In the 1880s galena or lead ore was discovered on Casper Mountain as was asbestos, gold, copper, and silver. With each strike, folks just shut down their Casper business house — boarded up the windows, and took off for the new ore fields! When the rainbow flickered and the boom played out, they came back, dusted off the shelves a bit, and opened the doors for business — as usual!

Still, there were several other booms Casper was noted for in the early days. When the Fremont, Elkhorn and Missouri Valley R.R. came into what is now Casper, a land boom took place. Cattle and sheep county records prove that in 1890 there were over 28,901 sheep and 28,029 cattle. Those figures boomed to 250,000 head of sheep in Natrona County with over 12,000 head of cattle in 1895.

But speaking of booms of an unusual character, you have to count the earthquake that took place there, too. On the darkest hour before dawn on June 25, 1894, an earthquake caused a great roaring and booming noise, threw people out of their beds, and generally scared the daylights out of them. No great damage was done outside of a few glasses here and there being broken.

Three years later, a really sharp earthquake hit Casper. Again local historians said a great rumbling and roaring with a regular quality was heard for minutes before it shook Casper residents at their breakfast on November 14, 1897.

Just about where the Yesness store is located downtown, the Grand Central Hotel was once located. It was said that a huge crack appeared in the walls of the old frame hotel, nearly splitting the building in half.

Men in the open prairies with their sheep and cattle reported a real booming quality to this earthquake.

The third such earthquake was reported in 1922, but was hardly noteworthy. Still, one newspaper writer said he heard a booming noise that day, so we count it as one of the unusual "booms" in Casper.

But the biggest and most unusual boom occurred on May 26, 1919. Three men were driving an auto-truck loaded down with 400 quarts of nitroglycerine from the Wyoming Torpedo Company to a small dugout storage on the east side of Casper near the present-day trap range.

The sweating driver had eased his load up and down narrow ruts with great deftness until the hard rubber tires of his vehicle slipped off the edge of a large chuck hole — and that is all she wrote! The explosion was heard for miles and gave Casper its largest boom in history.

Over three thousand people came out to look at the crater, and though they looked high and low, they found nothing of the three men, the auto-truck or, for that matter, the nitroglycerine that caused Casper's loudest boom!